MAKE YOUR HOME SAFE & SECURE

CONTENTS

EDITORIAL
Project Manager: Sandra Hartley
Project Editors: Marian Broderick,
Sheridan Carter
Craft Editor: Tonia Todman
Editorial Co-ordinator: Margaret Kelly
UK Editors: Martin Preston,
Andrew Kemp

TEXT
Alison Magney
Hugh Slatyer

DESIGN AND PRODUCTION
Tracey Burt
Erica Dale
Suzanne Elworthy
Chris Hatcher

PHOTOGRAPHY
Yanto Noriento
Andrew Elton

ILLUSTRATIONS
Hugh Slatyer
Jill McLeod

COVER
Frank Pithers (Design)
Andrew Elton (Photography)

PUBLISHER
Philippa Sandall

Published by
J.B.Fairfax Press Pty Ltd
80-82 McLachlan Avenue
Rushcutters Bay 2011

MAKE YOUR HOME
SAFE 'N' SECURE
Includes Index
ISBN 1 86343 009 1

Formatted by
J.B.Fairfax Press Pty Ltd
Output by Adtype, Sydney
Printed by Toppan Printing Co,
Hong Kong

Distributed by
J.B.Fairfax Press Ltd
9 Trinity Centre, Park Farm Estate
Wellingborough Northants
Ph: (0933) 402330
Fax: (0933) 402234

INTRODUCTION

This title in 'The Working Weekend Series' looks at the problems we all face in making our homes and our lives safer and more secure.

We cover everything you need to know about creating a secure, hazard-free home environment for you, your young children and your elderly relatives. We blend sound advice with easy-to-follow practical information. Look through our Contents page – you'll see there's no stone left unturned!

We go through an average home inside and out, room by room, dealing with everything from lighting, fences and alarm systems through to medicine storage and stair guards, electrical sockets and child-proof gate latches.

Our simple, illustrated instructions will give you the confidence you need to fit door locks, put up secure fencing, install safety catches on cupboards and the myriad do-it-yourself projects to do with security.

The book basically divides into two sections. The first deals with burglar-proofing your home and the second with accident-proofing it, with a particular emphasis on child-safety. We also have an emergency guide, and a section on how to deal with the hidden dangers in your home, such as poisons, and with other environmental concerns like recycling. Our simple checklists and projects can also be used by all those living alone, young or old, to whom security may be of special importance.

Let us help you make your home safe and secure for all family members to live in.

Do-it-yourself projects are satisfying. There's nothing to match that feeling of accomplishment, that little tinge of smugness, when you've done the job yourself and done it well! There are basic rules, however, which shouldn't be ignored or stampeded in your rush to get projects under way.

GETTING STARTED
Sorting out your priorities

O ne of the first rules is fairly obvious: you need to make lists of all the safety and security projects that need doing around your house and then put them in order of priority.

Allocate your time accordingly. Spending ages installing bars over upstairs windows could be seen as a waste of time if you have a just-crawling or just-walking baby and no stair guards, or an elderly relative who can't get out of the bath without assistance and with no grab rail installed!

Deal with the urgent, everyday security and safety problems first.

Let's start with a home security checklist. Sit down, armed with your most important weapons – pen and paper – and work out just where your home security is lacking.

Not all the points on the checklist will have a do-it-yourself project as a solution. Some points just need to be thought about, to make you more conscious of home security in general.

How to be more security conscious

SECURITY CHECKLIST

❑ An 'untamed' garden or excess 'bushiness' provides good hiding places and cover for burglars. Are your side paths or other entrances difficult to see, from either outside the home or inside it? Plant thorny or prickly plants in those areas that are vulnerable.

❑ How efficient is your external lighting system?

Is it fitted to time switches, so that it goes off during daylight hours? Is the garage area well lit too? Pathways? Lamps are available these days that light up when they 'sense' that someone is coming towards the house, and might be worth thinking about.

❑ Are your ground floor windows locked and the surrounds of sufficient quality to make 'jemmying' very difficult or impossible? Do low-level windows and glass doors contain laminated or shatterproof glass?

❑ Are your front, back and side doors really solid (at least 45 mm thick)? Are they fitted with deadlocks? 'Peephole' viewers? Safety chains? Do you deadlock your doors when you go out, so that if a burglar succeeds in getting in through a window, he or she is limited in what can be carried out?

❑ If you like leaving doors open to catch the breeze in summer, do you have a lockable metal security door which allows the breeze to come through? Do you leave doors or windows open when you're in the garden, having a nap, feeding the baby, 'just popping up to the shops' or on similar occasions?

❑ Do you have keys hidden outside the house, under doormats, under pot plants, in electricity boxes or anywhere else obvious? (Yes, obvious!)

❑ If the house is empty during working hours and even beyond, do you take measures to make the house appear occupied, such as leaving radios on or using timed light switches?

❑ Do you leave home at a set time every day? Can you alter your habits in any way, like having different lights programmed to come on each day and leaving the curtains in different positions so as to appear less predictable?

❑ Does your open garage advertise that you are out?

❑ Are valuables like videos or cameras near windows (smash-and-grab) or visible through windows or glass doors?

❑ Don't leave tools or ladders that could be used to 'break and enter' around the back or front of the house, even overnight.

❑ Don't have your name or address attached to your key ring.

❑ Is there a local Neighbourhood Watch scheme you could join? More about this on page 12.

❑ Why not ask a friend or spouse to try breaking into your house, or try it yourself? How easy is it?

❑ Get some quotes on having a security system installed, even if all you think you can afford is the very basic alarm. You may be pleasantly surprised. If the expense breaks your budget, ask if you can buy the metal box that fits over the alarm only, or perhaps just get hold of some of those 'These premises are protected by XYZ alarms' stickers. Both these ruses can be successful, not to mention cheap. There's no harm in asking!

❑ When you think you've covered everything, you're ready for the final item on the security checklist. Ask your local police station to send a crime-prevention officer to your house to go over your security arrangements. You'll be amazed at the loopholes an expert can find!

Keep your 'home sweet home' safe and secure

ABSOLUTE BASICS

Having established your security needs, and what needs doing most urgently, it's time to think about the practicalities.

Use a wheelbarrow or trolley to shift heavy items

Firstly, what tools will you need? Most homes should have the absolute basics, even if they are well hidden in the third drawer down in the kitchen cabinet, or the 'junk drawer'. Following is a list of what your basic tool kit should include:

☐ pliers
☐ screwdriver(s)
☐ chisel
☐ tape measure
☐ hammer

You'll need to add the following simple tools, then find a lockable storage box to put them all in:

☐ saws – one for small cuts (tenon saw) and one for large cuts (panel saw)
☐ a good quality pencil, or a craft knife, for making cut guidelines
☐ a 2-speed electric drill with various accessories accompanying it (no need to go overboard)
☐ a spirit level, or an ordinary level with plumb-line and bob
☐ a try square for measuring right angles
☐ adjustable spanner
☐ claw hammer
☐ bradawl for starting screw holes
☐ Stanley knife
☐ filling knife
☐ brick bolster
☐ plane

SAFETY GUIDE

With any job that involves using tools with which you are not all that familiar, and particularly any job that involves power tools, there are some safety considerations to keep in mind. Let's look at some general safety guidelines to consider when doing any of the do-it-yourself projects contained in this book.

✳ All power tools and their attachments should be double-insulated.

✳ Keep long hair, shirt tails or anything else that may flap around tied back so that they don't get caught up in fans or moving belts.

✳ Small children should not be 'helping' around ladders, sharp tools, loose panes of glass or any other do-it-yourself paraphernalia.

✳ Tighten loose hammer heads and axe heads.

✳ Remove nails from timber before you attempt to work with it or cut it.

✳ Pace yourself. You're asking for trouble if, for instance, you try to become an expert at

Avoid back problems by learning to lift properly

laying cement overnight. Take it slowly and do your aching limbs a favour.

✳ Avoid back problems by learning to lift properly. An upright back is best for most lifting jobs. Bend knees when picking up a weight from the ground. Put feet apart and one foot a little in front of the other. Don't stick out your chin as you lift; tuck it in.

✳ Share heavy loads where possible.

✳ Spade work needs some thought as well as muscle! When digging at Point A and moving sand or earth to Point B, make sure Points A and B are close together and do not require any twisting of your body. Take only half loads onto the spade.

✳ When shifting heavy items such as bags of fertiliser use a wheelbarrow or trolley.

✳ Avoid inhaling or being struck by minute particles of wood when sawing or sanding timbers. Wear a mask and goggles. Wear gloves, sensible shoes and sturdy clothes too, wherever possible.

✳ A simple way to secure a ladder is to tie the top of the ladder to vice grip pliers which are clamped onto the eaves gutter.

Don't let this happen while you're away! It's a sure giveaway to thieves that the owners are not in residence. Arrange to have your mail and papers collected regularly or have these services cancelled temporarily

HAPPY HOLIDAYS

Burglars don't take holidays! The excitement of getting away can prevent even the most security conscious person from thinking clearly. Here is a special holiday checklist which you might like to cut out and keep in your passport!

◾ Cancel newspapers, milk, laundry service and any other regular service – but do it discreetly. There is no need to tell people why you are dispensing with their services for the time being. Don't say how long you're dispensing with them either – just say 'until further notice'.

◾ Mow the lawn, trim the shrubbery and water the pot plants before you go so there are no visible signs of neglect from the street.

◾ Maybe a neighbour will agree to park his or her car in your driveway while you are away, assuming they have a garage themselves or are at home most of the time and can therefore protect themselves too.

◾ Make sure mail is collected, as well as junk mail, local newspapers, advertising leaflets and the other bits and pieces of paper that flow in an unending stream into our letter boxes and under our doors.

◾ Use your discretion about letting a neighbour have a set of your keys and about letting the police know you are going to be away. If you are the distrustful kind, do neither of these things.

◾ Burglars have been known to frequent check-in desks at airports and railway stations. Why? So that they can read luggage labels, find out what address you are temporarily leaving, and pay a visit there! Put your office address or a relative's office address on your luggage.

◾ If no-one can be trusted to collect your mail for you, or if you're going to be away for several weeks, have your mail redirected or held for you at the Post Office.

◾ A few kids' toys scattered around the front of the house makes it look busy and occupied. Just make sure you don't care if the toys disappear!

The word 'valuables' covers a wide, sometimes weird, assortment of items. To some people, nothing could be more valuable than the tattered envelope containing a lock of their child's hair; to others, value is inherent in the beauty of an object; to others still, value is measured in money.

PRECIOUS THINGS
Looking after your valuables

One criterion all valuables share is the extreme upset caused if they are lost or stolen.

✳ Most burglars are the smash-and-grab variety, quickly looking around a house or car for something that will instantly translate into money for them. The first step you must take in protecting what you value is to keep it all out of sight and away from windows.

✳ Make a list of the items you value and keep it at your office or somewhere you feel it will be safe. Why? Often homeowners who are burgled are so deeply upset and shocked that they cannot give accurate descriptions to police of what has been taken. Often, weeks after the report of the burglary has gone in to police and the insurance companies, victims remember some items that slipped their minds in the initial drama.

✳ Take photos of any special items. Let's face it, your 'solitaire diamond ring' is going to look like a million other rings to an overworked police force! But if you provide a clear photo of it, pointing out special features, the carat size, the inscription inside it and so on, your chances are better.

✳ For reasonable pictures of jewellery you need a good quality camera, colour film and some items you can put beside the pieces of jewellery to give some idea of scale.

Not all would-be thieves are unkempt. What better disguise than an official-looking uniform, or a business suit and a clipboard?

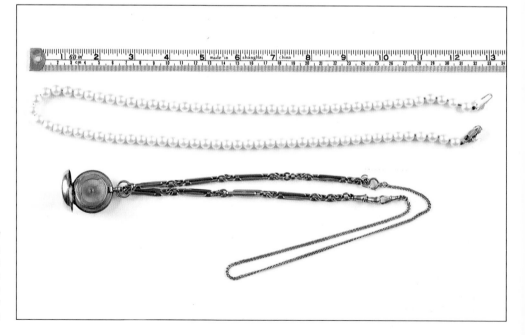

Take photographs of jewellery with a ruler or a matchbox in the picture as an indication of size. This is an accurate and acceptable method of identifying jewellery involved in household claims

You can, for instance, put a matchbox next to a ring or a video box along the length of a necklace so that police get an accurate picture of the size of the object.

✳ Items you should photograph, rather than attempt to describe, include collections of butterflies, stamps, coins, works of art, silver cutlery, trays, crystal, ornaments, clocks, important books and photo albums.

✳ Don't be embarrassed about listing and photographing the items that are of sentimental value, no matter how quirky it may seem.

✳ Don't store valuables in your bedroom as that is where a burglar will head for straight away. Think of somewhere really unusual, like in an envelope taped to the inside of an unused saucepan lid, deep in a messy and noisy saucepan cupboard.

✳ Keep one set of photos at home. Keep another set with your list of valuables.

✳ For larger items, like television sets, videos and compact disc players, recording the model name, brand and serial number is a good idea.

✳ The single most useful aid in the recovery and ultimate return of your valuables is to mark them permanently with security markers with your postcode followed by the house number.

✳ Security markers may be visible or invisible. Visible markers include permanent-ink fibre tip pens, diamond tip scribers

and electro-engravers. Invisible marker pens show up only under ultraviolet light, and police stations are now equipped with these light sources. Make a note of where each item has been marked.

✳ An extra deterrent when property has been marked is to display a 'warning' notice to that effect on your windows. Self-adhesive warning stickers are supplied with some markers.

✳ Engraving is the most permanent form of marking. Some items you may not think of engraving include:
☐ microwave oven
☐ sporting goods, like golf clubs and metal tennis racquets
☐ personal computer
☐ printer
☐ facsimile machine
☐ musical instruments
☐ binoculars
☐ valuable tables and chairs
☐ power tools
☐ lawn mower

INSURANCE

Insuring your property and your valuables is often expensive, but trying to start from scratch, if a burglar really cleans you out, would be horrendously expensive.

✳ Before contacting any insurers, go through each room in your house carrying a piece of paper and a pen. What would you want to or need to replace if a fire, flood or serious earthquake hit tomorrow and you were totally cleaned out? Make similar inventories for your tool shed, garage and

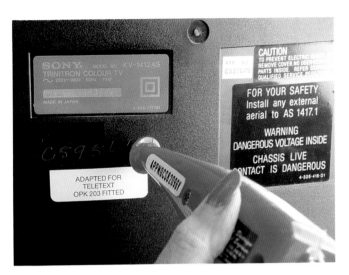

A hand-held electro-engraver is easily used to label portable electrical household goods. Check with your local authorities as to what is acceptable as an identifier

other outbuildings.

✳ Estimate what it would cost to buy everything again, at today's prices. That is the figure for which you should be insuring, as well as for the cost of rebuilding the house in the case of fire or earthquake.

✳ Armed with this list, and having added up the total monetary value, contact four or five insurance companies and ask for an estimate of their premium over the phone. Then ask for a copy of their application forms. Look these over with a jaundiced eye. What are the exclusions? Is a burst internal water-pipe flood covered and a natural flood not? Does the firm offer a discounted premium if you are part of a Neighbourhood Watch scheme? Will they insure without a full inspection of your security arrange-ments? Will they protect some things inside the house (like that diamond solitaire ring) and not

cover it if it's lost or stolen outside the house? Can you understand what the policy says, or is it written in 'legalese'? Will the firm's representative take time to explain fine points of detail, or are they only interested in getting you to sign on the dotted line?

✳ Ask friends and neighbours what insurance firm they use and, more importantly, how they've been treated if they've ever had to make a claim.

Floor safes are worth every effort, particularly if you are sentimentally attached to your jewellery, photos or other small items, or have a number of legal deeds that need to be kept safe from possible fire. You may just want the added security and convenience that a safe offers.

Project 1

Floor Safes

A floor safe offers excellent secure storage for valuables kept in the home as it is protected by the floor surrounding it. If you are building a new home, or extending your house, you should consider the inclusion of a floor safe.

Floor safes are, in effect, steel boxes with some form of protruding steel angle at the bottom to lock them into the surrounding concrete.

A floor safe can also be installed in a timber floor. Although it is not as secure as one built into a concrete floor, the timber makes it difficult for someone to get to the safe, even if they find it.

Locking systems can be either keyed or combination. The combination-type lock will come with a factory combination setting which you can change to any number you wish which is not easily forgotten, such as your birthdate.

The safe should be located out of sight under the stairs or in a storage area. Ideally, the location should make it easy for you to get to the contents of the safe while making it impossible for an intruder to use heavy tools to break it open. Under the stairs is a practical place as there is usually only enough room for the safe to be accessible but not enough to 'swing a hammer'.

The installation of a safe in a new house with a concrete floor is best left to a builder or structural engineer as it will be necessary to modify the design of the steel reinforcing.

The safe is simply cast into the concrete floor slab. Make sure that the top of the safe is covered with a heavy-duty plastic sheet, such as the underlay used under the slab, so that concrete does not spill onto the lock mechanism and door.

If the house or the new extension is to have a timber floor, the safe can be set into a pad of concrete below floor level. If you are going to install a safe below an existing timber floor, start by locating the existing floor joists. These will be evident by the rows of nails securing the floorboards.

STEP BY STEP

1   Select a safe which will fit between the joists so that the amount of cutting and trimming is reduced. A common safe size is 300 mm

x 300 mm internally with an overall external measurement of 370 mm, which is small enough to fit between two joists.

2   Space floor joists at 450 mm, centre to centre, leaving 400 mm clear between the joists.

3   Cut the floorboards along the joint lines so that the saw cuts are approximately 450 mm apart and for a length of 450 mm. The spacing of the cuts may not be exactly 450 mm but will depend on the floor joint spacing. Similarly, cut across the boards, centred on the joists below, so that you have a cut square hole that is approximately 450 mm x 450 mm.

4   Cut the floorboards using a power saw with the blade depth set slightly deeper than the floorboards – 20 mm should be enough. Put the floorboards which you have cut out aside, for the access panel.

5   Once the opening is formed, cut two trimming joists and fix between the main joists using joist-hangers. This will be easier than trying to nail into the main joists.

6   All that remains now is to form up a square to enclose the concrete pad into which the safe is set, with at least 100 mm of concrete all around. Make sure that the safe is not placed too low

---

WHAT TO BUY
- [ ] 100 mm x 50 mm hardwood, 1 m (trimming joists)
- [ ] old plywood (formwork for concrete)
- [ ] 12 mm thick ply
- [ ] 75 mm x 25 mm planed battens, 1 m long (access panel)
- [ ] ready-mixed concrete, approximately 2 bags

TOOLS
- [ ] power saw

TIME
Allow one day

below the floor and that the door opens without catching on the floor framing.

7 Place half-bricks at the bottom to rest the safe on. Use ready-mixed concrete which is available in bags from your hardware store. Pour into the base and tamp or pack it down with a stick to make sure that it fills the formwork. When the base is formed, place the safe in position and cover the top with a plastic sheet secured with masking tape. Proceed to pour concrete around the sides of the safe, again using a stick to tamp the concrete well into place.

8 Use plywood trimming panels between the top of the safe and the floor framing.

9 The access panel is made using the floorboards which were cut out. Clamp these together face down and screw two timber battens across the boards. Fit a flush-fitting ring-pull on to the upper face of the access panel.

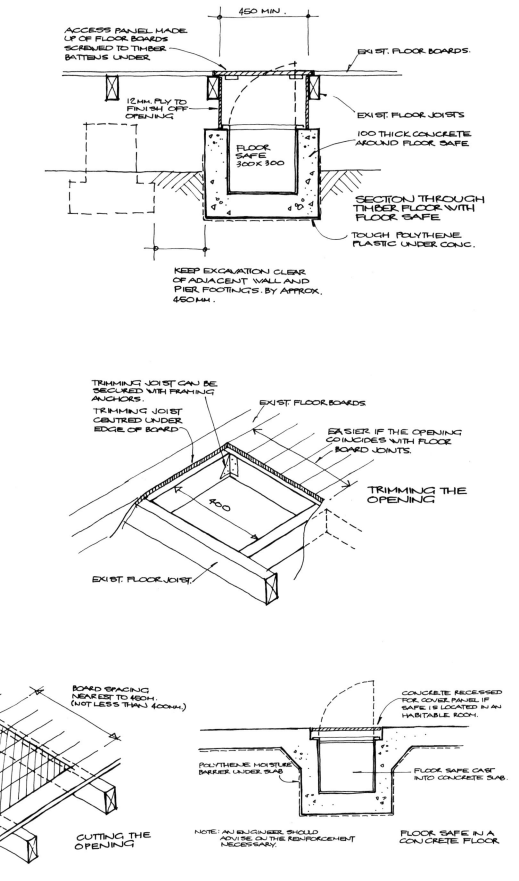

450 MIN.

ACCESS PANEL MADE UP OF FLOOR BOARDS SCREWED TO TIMBER BATTENS UNDER

EXIST. FLOOR BOARDS.

12 MM. PLY TO FINISH OFF OPENING

EXIST. FLOOR JOISTS

FLOOR SAFE 300 × 300

100 THICK CONCRETE AROUND FLOOR SAFE

SECTION THROUGH TIMBER FLOOR WITH FLOOR SAFE

TOUGH POLYTHENE PLASTIC UNDER CONC.

KEEP EXCAVATION CLEAR OF ADJACENT WALL AND PIER FOOTINGS. BY APPROX. 450 MM.

TRIMMING JOIST CAN BE SECURED WITH FRAMING ANCHORS.

TRIMMING JOIST CENTRED UNDER EDGE OF BOARD

EXIST. FLOOR BOARDS

EASIER IF THE OPENING COINCIDES WITH FLOOR BOARD JOINTS.

TRIMMING THE OPENING

400

EXIST. FLOOR JOIST.

JOIST SPACING APPROX. 450MM.

BOARD SPACING NEAREST TO 450M. (NOT LESS THAN 400MM.)

CUTTING THE OPENING

CONCRETE RECESSED FOR COVER PANEL IF SAFE IS LOCATED IN AN HABITABLE ROOM.

POLYTHENE MOISTURE BARRIER UNDER SLAB

FLOOR SAFE CAST INTO CONCRETE SLAB.

NOTE: AN ENGINEER SHOULD ADVISE ON THE REINFORCEMENT NECESSARY.

FLOOR SAFE IN A CONCRETE FLOOR

Retreating into a fortressed world of bars, burglar alarms, deadlocks, four door chains, weapons and perpetually peckish Dobermans is one home security option. It is an unattractive option which reflects the desperation many people feel in their anxiety to protect family and property.

GOOD NEIGHBOURS

Be a part of your community

I n recent years, there has been a growth in popularity of the more sensible security option of involving the community in collective responsibility for what goes on within its environs.

This collective responsibility idea is known by a number of names, such as Home Watch, Community Watch, Tower Watch – but most commonly Neighbourhood Watch.

The principles involved are much the same around the world. People in a neighbourhood or in some similarly defined area decide to keep an eye on things and report anything unusual to each other and to the local police. It's as simple as that, but the impact of such schemes on crime statistics has been most impressive.

The Safety House scheme also involves community participation, providing a refuge for people in danger. Children should be taught to recognise the Safety House symbol and know that it is somewhere that they can go to for help if in danger.

SETTING UP A SCHEME

Anywhere from 30 to 800 homes, including flats, townhouses and so on, can be considered a suitable number for the setting up of a scheme. The actual number in any one scheme is usually governed by natural boundaries. For instance, the homes around a square might belong to one scheme while those in adjacent streets might belong to other schemes. Obviously, surveillance around corners rather defeats the object!

Become involved in protecting your neighbourhood – when you join your local Watch group you are never completely on your own, there is always help nearby.

Security warning signs will tell any would-be thief that he is likely to be watched! They are supplied by local watch groups when you become a member, and are best positioned in a prominent window near an entrance

Similarly, a block of flats would probably form a single Watch area.

Ideally, the people in each scheme should know each other either by sight or by name. A committee is formed consisting of police officers and residents, again ideally, including long-term residents who know more about the area than anybody else. Occasional meetings are held to discuss procedures and generally keep in touch.

Most people find there is plenty to be enthusiastic about when their property and family's safety is on the line. Even the cagiest people, who are usually concerned about their privacy, can see the benefits of exchanging

work and home telephone numbers with neighbours and of letting them know of holiday plans, or when a TV or household appliance is being delivered.

You can get a Watch scheme started just by going around your block of flats or street drumming up enthusiasm. Once you feel there is enough interest for a good attendance at a public meeting, arrange one for a time that suits the local police station. Then they can attend and set things up officially.

In some places, the police prefer to see a petition of signatures of interested parties before they set aside a time and place for a public meeting.

In still other places, police will send a kit of information after just one interested party makes an enquiry.

One of the greatest visible benefits of having an official scheme set up is the distribution of official logos. Posted in public places, with mini-versions being attached in a prominent position to windows, these logos announce to all prospective burglars that they are in an area where 'I don't want to become involved' is not in the residents' vocabulary.

People who participate in Neighbourhood Watch schemes don't spend half their waking hours calling in the police to check out suspicious moving vans.

The police should only be contacted if, after contacting every number on your list for a particular house and being unable to reach anyone, your suspicions of really unusual behaviour justify calling in the local police.

Any obviously criminal activity should be reported to police immediately. Keep the local police station's number where you can reach it quickly. Keep scrap paper and pens in an easily reached place so that you can take down a car description, number plate or other details in a rush. It's better not to rely on memory alone at times like these.

Once upon a time, in what now seems like a fairyland, everybody knew everybody else in the neighbourhood and looked out for each other's interests. The modern replacement is Neighbourhood Watch.

Left: Shops in the hub of your suburban shopping centre are ideal bases for a Safety House, identified here by a larger-than-usual sticker. Our caring community pharmacist, with his shop across from the railway station is an ideal Safety House location

Above: The warning sticker on this house door may act as a deterrent in itself to a would-be intruder

It is a truism that the basis of any security measure is to make your house or flat appear more difficult to break into. Make external security a priority by dealing with doors, windows, external lighting, paths, fences and alarms.

EXTERNAL SECURITY
The first line of defence

Good fences, noisy paths, safe doors and smart windows are all deterrents to a would-be thief. Look at our security ideas and refer to our suggestions on External Lighting on page 16.

Security bars over the double doors of this inner city terrace house provide an effective barrier offering much greater resistance to attack.

Good outside lighting makes excellent sense. Apart from preventing pedestrian accidents at night, it's a good deterrent to prowlers or thieves. Ideally, dual controls should be installed so that switches can be used from the garage or driveway. Be sure to use strong light bulbs in fittings, and approach lighting design with both safety and aesthetic appeal in mind

Even the sight of an alarm positioned prominently on the house acts as a dissuasion to thieves. Some alarms can be installed by a handyperson and, with controls just inside the front door, are easy to operate

Our furry friend is a valuable deterrent to would-be intruders. A loud bark is enough to warn any thief that he has opposition

It's often said that thieves operate 'under cover of darkness' and darkness does indeed provide a protective mantle over people up to no good. Adequate street lighting and bright lights around your house are likely to take that protective mantle away from prowlers.

EXTERNAL LIGHTING

G ood external lighting can help deter many an opportunist burglar. Study your property carefully to establish firstly what areas you want to light up, such as the entry and front path, and secondly the areas where someone is likely to hide, such as behind shrubs, dark corners or beside the house.

If you have a semi-detached house, the main areas for security lighting is the front entry area and the rear garden.

External lighting may consist of spotlights or wall lights switched from inside, or include passive infra-red detectors which turn lights on when someone passes by.

Another alternative is to have the switching for these external lights connected to a master switch so that all external lights can be turned on at once. Would-be intruders are more unlikely to go anywhere near a well-lit house.

Also, if the house is guarded with an internal alarm system, outside lighting allows the

For adequate street lighting, you'll have to lobby your local council. Your home, however, is _your_ business. Basically, the brighter your lights are, the better, particularly if they are well maintained and have been thoughtfully and strategically placed.

intruder to see the warning signs, thereby leaving the house intact.

At a minimum expense, entry points such as doors and windows should be spotlit.

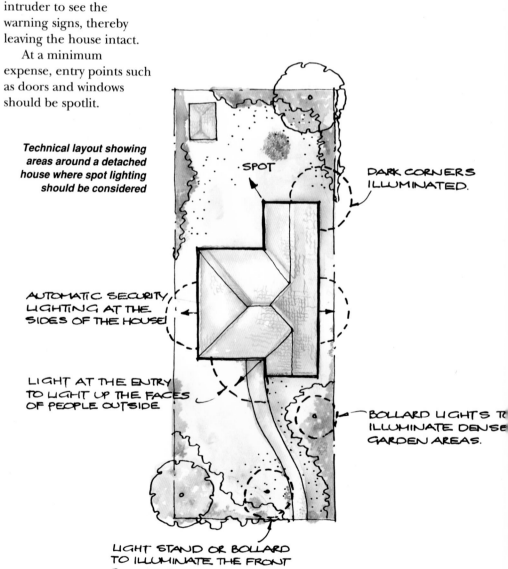

Technical layout showing areas around a detached house where spot lighting should be considered

SPOT

DARK CORNERS ILLUMINATED.

AUTOMATIC SECURITY LIGHTING AT THE SIDES OF THE HOUSE

LIGHT AT THE ENTRY TO LIGHT UP THE FACES OF PEOPLE OUTSIDE

BOLLARD LIGHTS T ILLUMINATE DENSE GARDEN AREAS.

LIGHT STAND OR BOLLARD TO ILLUMINATE THE FRONT BOUNDARY AREA

An effective way of providing security to the grounds of a semi-detached house, or one on a small block of land, is to lay this gravel perimeter path at the side of the house.

Project 2

Gravel Paths

A gravel path acts as a deterrent in two ways: the noise of someone on the gravel will alert you to an intruder, but a would-be thief is more likely to take note of this and be put off.

All you will need for this project are long lengths of timber edging, short timber stakes and your own selection of gravel. The gravel should consist of lumps of stone which are about 10 mm in diameter so that the path will not eventually compact together into a hard surface – this would defeat the purpose of the whole exercise. Gravel can be purchased through a landscaping or builders' merchant company.

The timber should be able to resist insect attack, where this is likely, and wet rot. Appropriate timber for the edging is either hardwood, naturally durable cedar, or preservative-impregnated softwood such as pine.

The only tools you need are a saw and hammer and galvanised flat head nails for fixing the edging to the stakes.

STEP BY STEP

1 To be effective, the path should extend from the side wall of the house to within approximately 150 mm of the side fence. This will provide just enough room to plant small shrubs or vines without allowing extra room for an intruder to bypass the gravel.

2 Dig a shallow trench for the edging. Next use a string line to set out the line for the stakes.

3 Hammer the stakes into the ground about 900 mm apart. Nail the timber edging to the stakes with joints centred at a stake. Drill for all nails near the ends of the boards so as to prevent splitting of the timber.

4 If the ground is damp clay the gravel may slowly sink into the clay. The clay in turn would rise up into the gravel and reduce the amount of noise it makes when walked on. If this is likely, the ground should be prepared first by spreading a layer of well compacted hardcore about 38 mm to 50 mm thick. Make sure this is well bedded down by tamping and rolling.

5 Finally, spread the gravel with a rake so it is a little higher than the edging at the middle of the path. When the gravel settles it will then sit flush to the edging.

TIMBER PEGS TO SECURE EDGE BOARD. SPACING APPROX. 900 APPROX. 200 LONG.

TIMBER EDGE BOARD 75 × 25

RIVER GRAVEL APPROX. 50 mm DEEP.

GROUND SHOULD BE FIRM, NOT CLAY. LAY CRUSHED ROCK SUB-BASE IF CLAY IS ENCOUNTERED.

75

50

WHAT TO BUY

- ☐ 75 mm x 25 mm hardwood (cedar) or preservative-impregnated softwood (pine), quantity depends on length of path
- ☐ 38 mm x 38 mm hardwood or softwood, allow 1 m length for each 6 m length of path
- ☐ 50 of 2.5 mm long galvanised round head nails (500 per kg)
- ☐ blue metal, allow 0.5 cubic m per ton plus 10% for wastage

TOOLS

- ☐ power saw
- ☐ string line

TIME

Allow half an hour per metre

'Good fences make good neighbours' a wise person once said, but they can be a double-edged sword if they protect burglars from view. Follow our guidelines for sensible fencing.

Project 3

Picket Fencing

STEP BY STEP

1 When setting out the fence, start by fixing a string line along the line of the fence. Use a crowbar and post-hole borer to dig the holes for the posts.
The posts can be between 1800 mm and 2400 mm apart. After placing the posts into the holes, temporarily prop them plumb and check that they are in line with the string.

2 Check the line of the top of the posts. Start with the two end posts and pull a string line between the tops of these two posts. The tops of the intermediate posts should be in line with this string.

3 Fix the fence rails into the posts and check the line of the posts afterwards. When the rails are fixed in place the post holes can be filled with concrete. Leave the temporary propping in place until the concrete is set.

4 When the concrete has set and cured for at least a day, the pickets can be fixed to the rails. Cut a piece of timber to a width to match the spacing between the rails and use this as a template when fixing the pickets. Once the first picket is fixed plumb it will be easier to fix the rest plumb using the template.

5 Pickets should be fixed with galvanised round head

Fencing materials such as pickets, rails and posts can be purchased precut, complete with prefabricated gates, from specialist companies. In some cases the fence panels can be bought preassembled ready to set into the posts. Timbers are vacuum-impregnated with preservative as protection against wet rot and insect attack.

nails 50 mm long, with two nails at each crossing. Use a spirit level to check for plumb as you proceed.

Top: The charm of picket fences is emphasised in this situation. The variety of greens in the garden causes this fence to blend in well

Right: Timeless stone fences may take more effort to create – and they certainly cost more, but they are enduring and have a graciousness of their own. Local quarried stone, cut into even blocks is shown here, but don't overlook re-using stone foundation blocks or uneven pieces joined for a more informal look

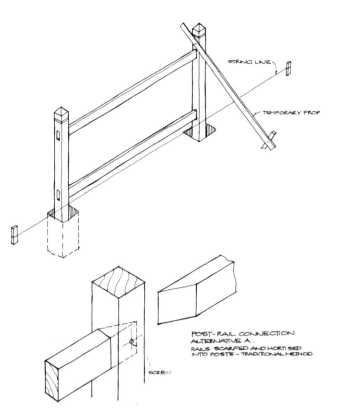

STRING LINE

TEMPORARY PROP

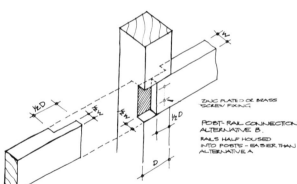

POST-RAIL CONNECTION
ALTERNATIVE A.
RAILS SCARFED AND MORTISED
INTO POSTS – TRADITIONAL METHOD.

SCREW

ZINC PLATED OR BRASS
SCREW FIXING

POST-RAIL CONNECTION
ALTERNATIVE B.
RAILS HALF HOUSED
INTO POSTS – EASIER THAN
ALTERNATIVE A

These made-to-order fence panels replace the rotten timber slats previously there between the stone fence supports. This fence is a good example of a high, secure fence which still provides vision to the street

TO WIDE PICKETS
SET APPROX 65
APART.

100 x 100 DRESSED
POST EQUAL
SPACING UP TO
2400 APART.

100 x 50 DRESSED
FENCE RAILS

⅓ H BUT NOT
LESS THAN 300

DIG HOLE 100
BIGGER THAN
POST ALL ROUND
SET POST IN CONCRETE

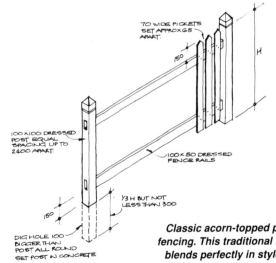

Classic acorn-topped picket fencing. This traditional fence blends perfectly in style and colour with the equally traditional house it is protecting

Doors are often of inferior quality, to be broken down with one strong kick. Locks and latches are only as good as the base door you have, so keep that in mind and buy the best quality entry door you can afford.

Project 4

Door Locks and Latches

MORTISE LOCKS

Strong door locks and latches are vital to good security and peace of mind and are, in fact, very easy to install. Locks and bolts should be fitted to all vulnerable entry points.

The mortise lock is the best type of lock to install on an external door and is so called due to the fact that it fits into a recess cut into the edge of the door. For this reason they are much more secure than a lock fixed to the face of the door.

Common spring locks are a definite no-no for all external doors. They are the easiest and quickest type of lock to force open.

It is important to fit good locks to all doors and to easily accessible windows.

Door locks vary; some being designed for maximum protection while others are meant only for limited security.

Make sure you purchase your pin locks or latches from reputable locksmiths who are able to advise you on the best form of lock for your situation.

STEP BY STEP

1 Hold the lock against the side of the door and mark the position of the lock body, the handlebar (handlespindle) and keyhole.

2 Bore holes for the handlebar and keyhole. Use a brace and bit to bore a series of holes for the mortise along the centre of the door edge.

3 Use a piece of tape on the drill bit to mark the depth of the lock. The door should be secured from moving by slipping a chisel or timber wedge underneath.

4 Clean up the mortise with a sharp chisel. Insert the lock, with the bolt extended, and mark the outline of the faceplate.

5 Chisel a recess for the depth of the faceplate and again insert the lock and screw to the edge of the door.

6 Slip the handlebars through the side hole and fix the handles. Close the door against the frame and mark the location of the striker plate.

7 Cut a recess in the door frame for the plate and for the latch and bolt. Fit the striker plate in position.

WHAT TO BUY
Selected latch complete with screws and handles

TOOLS
☐ square
☐ brace and bit – bit size to suit width of lock

TIME
1-2 hours

Locks and latches, bought from reputable locksmiths, should be fitted to all external doors and accessible windows

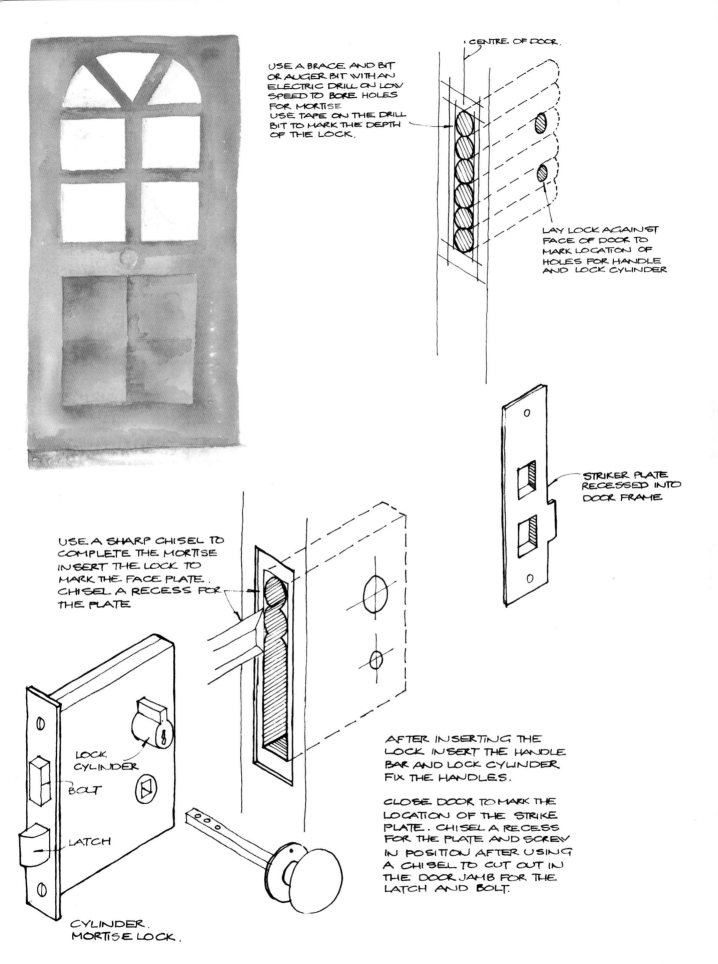

USE A BRACE AND BIT
OR AUGER BIT WITH AN
ELECTRIC DRILL ON LOW
SPEED TO BORE HOLES
FOR MORTISE
USE TAPE ON THE DRILL
BIT TO MARK THE DEPTH
OF THE LOCK.

CENTRE OF DOOR.

LAY LOCK AGAINST
FACE OF DOOR TO
MARK LOCATION OF
HOLES FOR HANDLE
AND LOCK CYLINDER

STRIKER PLATE
RECESSED INTO
DOOR FRAME

USE A SHARP CHISEL TO
COMPLETE THE MORTISE
INSERT THE LOCK TO
MARK THE FACE PLATE.
CHISEL A RECESS FOR
THE PLATE

LOCK
CYLINDER

BOLT

LATCH

CYLINDER.
MORTISE LOCK.

AFTER INSERTING THE
LOCK INSERT THE HANDLE
BAR AND LOCK CYLINDER
FIX THE HANDLES.

CLOSE DOOR TO MARK THE
LOCATION OF THE STRIKE
PLATE. CHISEL A RECESS
FOR THE PLATE AND SCREW
IN POSITION AFTER USING
A CHISEL TO CUT OUT IN
THE DOOR JAMB FOR THE
LATCH AND BOLT.

MORTISE LATCHES

This project features an inexpensive type of door latch, usually used for internal doors. The simple tube shape of the cylinder mortise latch makes it much simpler to install than a mortise lock.

WHAT TO BUY

TOOLS

☐ brace and bit – bit size to suit mortise latch

TIME

1-2 hours

Cylinder mortise latches can be bought with a snib lock to prevent turning of the handles but will offer little problem to a determined intruder.

STEP BY STEP

1 Mark the location of the lock and handlebars by placing the latch on the face of the door: mark the handlebar holes and centre line of the latch.

2 Transfer the mark for the centre line of the latch to the edge of the door.

3 Use a brace and bit to bore a hole for the latch. Insert the latch and mark the outline of the faceplate.

4 Chisel out a recess for the faceplate and insert and fix the latch.

5 The striker plate is fixed in the same way as the mortise lock. The striker plate is placed on the door jamb and an outline drawn around it.

6 Carefully chisel out for the depth of the plate and where the latch bolt sits. Screw until striker is in place.

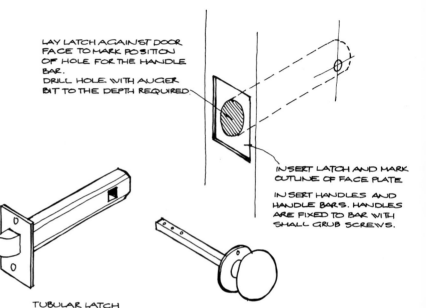

LAY LATCH AGAINST DOOR FACE TO MARK POSITION OF HOLE FOR THE HANDLE BAR.
DRILL HOLE WITH AUGER BIT TO THE DEPTH REQUIRED.

INSERT LATCH AND MARK OUTLINE OF FACE PLATE

INSERT HANDLES AND HANDLE BARS. HANDLES ARE FIXED TO BAR WITH SMALL GRUB SCREWS.

TUBULAR LATCH

STRIKER RECESSED INTO DOOR FRAME

Folding glass doors are a security risk and simply installing a door lock will not provide sufficient protection. Here this inner city terrace house has a concertina steel screen door to provide extra security

Never open your door until you've identified the caller. Friend or foe?
A door viewer is an essential and very basic security device. A must
for working parents with school-age children who beat them home!

Door Viewer

This is a small metal tube with a fish-eye lens through which you can see outside, with up to 180° field of view. Viewers are available from most hardware stores and are easy to install.

Don't forget that you must have a light which will illuminate people at the door – don't put the light behind them.

STEP BY STEP

1 Start by marking the position for the viewer on the outside of the door.

2 Use an auger drill bit, of the size specified by the viewer manufacturer, to drill

Installing a door viewer is a very easy and inexpensive project, one that enables you to quickly identify your caller without opening the door. Increased crime rates makes a door viewer an absolute necessity.

a hole through the door. Be careful that you stop when the end of the drill just shows through the door, and finish the hole from the other side. This prevents the door face from splitting.

3 The viewer consists of two tubes which screw together and enable the viewer to be used for a range of door thicknesses. From the outside of the door, insert the viewer into the hole. From the inside of the door, screw the other tube end into the viewer.

WHAT TO BUY

TOOLS

☐ speed drill bit to suit diameter of viewer, or brace and bit

TIME

1 hour

TIPSTRIP

■ Does everyone in the family know where the keys are to a deadlocked door or to key-locked windows? In the event of a fire, these keys should be immediately accessible.

■ The locksmith should arrive as the removal people leave. Change any window and door key-operated locks as soon as you buy or rent a new home.

■ If in a block of flats, a strategically placed mirror will ensure an intruder is not able to hide him or herself against the wall beside the door without being seen.

■ When fitting the door viewer remember that it is best installed in the middle of the door at eye height.

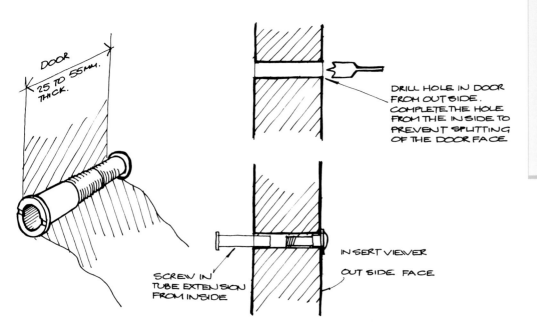

DOOR 25 TO 55mm. THICK.

DRILL HOLE IN DOOR FROM OUTSIDE. COMPLETE THE HOLE FROM THE INSIDE TO PREVENT SPLITTING OF THE DOOR FACE

SCREW IN TUBE EXTENSION FROM INSIDE

INSERT VIEWER OUTSIDE FACE

The vast majority of burglars not blessed with an open door don't have to look far before they find an open window (usually in the bathroom) in most houses.

Project 6

Window Bolts

DOUBLE HUNG WINDOWS

The easiest type of window to lock is the double-hung sash window. These windows are best secured with a dual screw available from hardware specialists or at some hardware stores.

Windows should always be locked, and ground floor windows should often be barred as well. Minimise the burglar's chances with the following projects.

This simple method of locking your windows gives double safety. The screw-in bolt is positioned and removed by a removable key, and once this is in place, a simple slide bolt increases the security. Both screw and bolt slide through to the outside window

STEP BY STEP

1 A hole is bored through the inner sash to suit the size of the outer barrel. A smaller hole is bored into the outer sash to take the inner security screw.

2 The outer threaded barrel is screwed into the inner sash so that the face is flush with the face of the timber sash. You will need a large screwdriver or, if this is not available, try the end of a steel square.

3 To lock the window, simply screw the inner security bolt into the outer barrel with a special key, so that it locks into the hole in the outer sash.

4 It is a good idea to drill two holes at the side of the outer sash, about 100 mm apart, so that the window can be locked in an open position for ventilation.

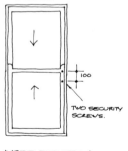

100

TWO SECURITY SCREWS.

INSIDE ELEVATION OF DOUBLE HUNG WINDOW

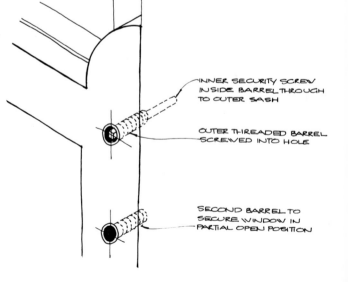

INNER SECURITY SCREW INSIDE BARREL THROUGH TO OUTER SASH

OUTER THREADED BARREL SCREWED INTO HOLE

SECOND BARREL TO SECURE WINDOW IN PARTIAL OPEN POSITION

CASEMENT AND HOPPER WINDOWS

A simple and neat mortise bolt is available for locking both casement and hopper windows as illustrated. If the window is large, fit two bolts.

WHAT TO BUY

TOOLS
- [ ] speed drill bit to suit diameter

TIME
Approximately 1 hour

STEP BY STEP

1 Place the mortise bolt against the inside face of the window sash to mark the position of the bolt on the sash, and the locking plate on the window frame. You also need to mark the location of the hole for the key.

2 Use a brace and bit or auger drill bit in an electric drill to bore a hole into the edge of the window sash. Be careful to not bore the hole too deep as the end of the drill bit may catch the edge of the glass and crack it. Drill a hole for the key only as deep as the hole for the bolt.

3 Fit the mortise bolt into the hole, with the bolt extended, and mark the face-plate profile. Use a chisel to neatly cut out for the face-plate. Fit the mortise bolt in position and screw the face-plate to the edge of the sash. Insert the key and make sure that it can turn easily, then screw the key plate to the face of the window sash.

4 The only thing remaining is to fit the locking plate to the window frame. Close the window and operate the bolt to mark the frame. Place the locking plate on the frame and mark the outline. Chisel out the frame to take the locking plate. Drill out a hole to take the locking bolt then, when this is done, screw the locking plate to the frame. Make sure that the locking bolt moves easily into the locking plate when you turn the key.

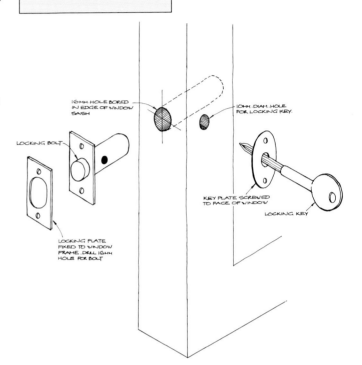

16MM HOLE BORED IN EDGE OF WINDOW SASH

10MM. DIAM. HOLE FOR LOCKING KEY.

LOCKING BOLT

KEY PLATE SCREWED TO FACE OF WINDOW

LOCKING KEY

LOCKING PLATE FIXED TO WINDOW FRAME. DRILL 16MM HOLE FOR BOLT

LOUVRE WINDOWS

Traditional glass louvre windows are the easiest windows to break into. An intruder only has to quietly slip out several glass blades to gain entry without warning neighbours. The only solution for this type of window is either to install security louvre blades or fit a different type of window sash.

Security louvre windows have metal inserts in the bladeholders which are bonded to the glass during installation and prevent it from being lifted out. The blade-holders are also protected from hacksaw attack by hardened steel pins and have a strong locking action.

For extra protection in high-risk areas, burglar bars can be fitted. These are made of mild steel rods and are fitted internally, one per blade, to provide a physical barrier in the event of glass breakage.

Louvre windows may be convenient for those narrow, difficult corners – but make sure they are not a security risk

Barred windows can serve a dual purpose: they keep unwanted intruders out and tiny members of the family in!

Project 7

Window Bars

Security bars and grilles on windows and doors are probably the most effective means of putting a burglar off. Security bars

All too often, bars are fitted only after a house has been broken into. Some insurance companies may insist on this type of security measure, especially in a high-risk area. This project covers two basic types of barred windows.

are not only a physical barrier but act as a visual deterrent as well. Indeed in many areas they are an unfortunate necessity.

Security bars are fabricated from mild steel vertical bars welded to steel crossbars. The completed frames should be hot-dipped galvanised to protect against corrosion.

The vertical bars are usually spaced at the width of a clenched fist – about

100 mm. Fabrication is usually beyond the facilities and skills of the weekend handyperson and should be carried out by engineering companies who specialise in this scale and type of work.

Two basic types of security bars are used. The

first is the traditional method where the crossbars are set into the joints of the brick wall. The second and simpler method uses a perimeter frame which has holes drilled for bolting to the wall using expanding masonry bolts. The

Internal bars on windows are often the only way of securing windows. These custom-made bars are constructed from stainless steel and screw to the internal window frame. The screws are later concealed with rubber plugs inserted into the screw-hole – thus making removal difficult indeed

advantage of this type is that the crossbars don't have to be accurately aligned with the brick joints.

STEP BY STEP

1 Fitting the crossbars, however, is not beyond the handyperson. If you are fitting the traditional bars, the brick joints to take the crossbars will have to be cleaned out. In old houses the mortar will be relatively soft lime mortar and can easily be raked out with a small cold chisel, screwdriver or a masonry drill. More modern houses will have been built with much harder mortar consisting of cement and sand. This type of mortar will have to be drilled out with a masonry drill.

2 When the crossbars have been pushed into the brick joint, point up the joint with cement mortar. Make sure that the mortar is not too wet but just moist. This will make it easier to push the mortar into the joint and ensure that it does not shrink and later become loose.

3 If you are fitting the second type involving a perimeter frame, use 10 mm expanding masonry anchors at least 50 mm long. For added security the bolt heads can be tack-welded to the perimeter frame.

The security bars illustrated are for an external location, which is fine for windows which don't open out. If you have windows with sashes which open out, bars with a perimeter frame can be fitted on the inside and fixed to the window frame with large cross-head screws

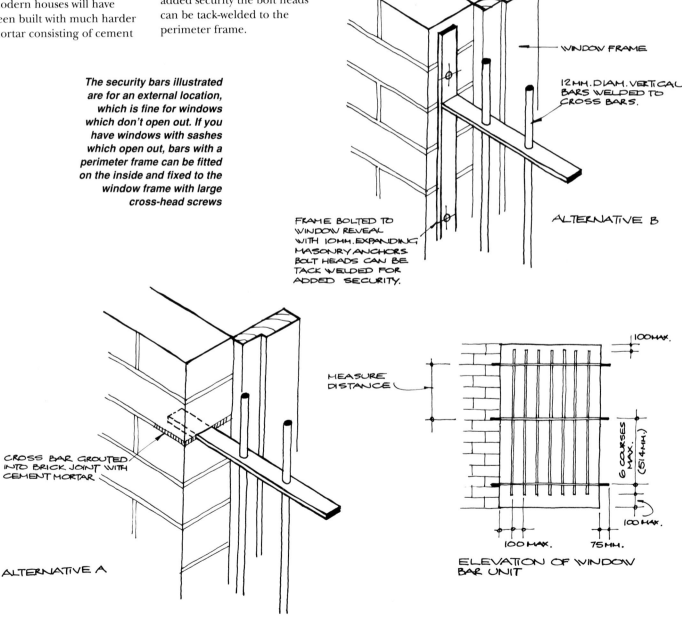

WINDOW FRAME

12 MM. DIAM. VERTICAL BARS WELDED TO CROSS BARS.

ALTERNATIVE B

FRAME BOLTED TO WINDOW REVEAL WITH 10MM. EXPANDING MASONRY ANCHORS BOLT HEADS CAN BE TACK WELDED FOR ADDED SECURITY.

CROSS BAR GROUTED INTO BRICK JOINT WITH CEMENT MORTAR

ALTERNATIVE A

MEASURE DISTANCE

100 MAX.

6 COURSES MAX. (514 MM.)

100 MAX.

100 MAX.   75 MM.

ELEVATION OF WINDOW BAR UNIT

Many rooms in the average home are accidents waiting to happen. Once children arrive, minor accidents and mishaps you would not have believed possible can become daily events.

SAFETY IN THE HOME
Accident-proofing your home

I t's our job as responsible homeowners to minimise the consequences of some of these inevitable hiccups, for our children, our elderly relatives, our friends, domestic help and visiting tradespeople.

We must also concentrate on preventing those accidents which are not hiccups, but potentially serious, even life-endangering ones.

Included in this part of the book are suggestions for child-proofing and checklists for the elderly.

Remember the old adage: out of sight is out of mind. Keeping hazards out of the way of curious youngsters is the best technique for kid's safety.

With intelligent planning many of the accidents that occur in the home can be avoided.

It's a simple fact of life that you can't always be there on the spot to protect and help – but you can do everything possible to prevent an accident from happening in the first place.

CHILDREN
A baby at the put-everything-into-the-mouth stage must have the barrier of distance put in its way. If the baby can't reach the pins, coins, buttons and other choking hazards of the average

house, it's not going to get into trouble – at least not that way!

Other barriers are playpens, pool fences, safety plugs in electrical outlets, laminated glass, fan guards, stove guards over hotplates – there are as many barriers to think about as there are potential accidents. So, if young children are around, you have to start thinking with a kind of siege mentality, because

the simple fact of life is, you can't always be there to explain, to distract, to protect, to help, or to satisfy their curiosity.

THE ELDERLY
To prevent accidents with the elderly, you have to think in terms of their limitations (such as poorer eyesight, diminished agility and so on) and in terms of providing simple solutions or aids that will make their limitations less

Let's face it, a happy, healthy family means peace of mind – and that really matters in a hectic family and work schedule

limiting! For example, an easily switched on, easily reached bedside light, or a bright, lightweight torch, makes getting up in the middle of the night safer for elderly people.

Many elderly people wear bifocals which can, for some, actually be disorienting, and cause giddiness and falls. Non-slip rugs, grip rails and other solutions, plus regular visits to the optician, can minimise risk. Where balance is a problem, aids like a chair in the shower, and a grip rail beside the toilet, can be a great help.

For many elderly people, a large part of their daily routine revolves

around taking medicines. For those suffering from poor memory, the question 'Did I take my 10 a.m. blood pressure pill or not?' is unanswerable. You can help here by buying a simple gadget from the chemist that stores pills according to the time of day they are to be taken. The 6 a.m. slot may have half a dozen pills in it, the 10 a.m. slot one pill, the noon slot four pills, and so forth, which means that once the gadget is 'loaded' (usually once a week), then remembering

To avoid a scene like this, it is advisable for all ground level windows to have safety laminated glass

EMERGENCY TELEPHONE LIST

Dial _____ for police, fire, or medical emergencies
(check telephone directory for local number)

Our address: _____

_____

_____

Nearest cross street: _____

Our telephone number: _____

Mum's telephone (work): _____ **Dad's telephone (work):** _____

Doctor: _____ at _____

Pediatrician: _____ at _____

Dentist: _____ at _____

24-hr pharmacy: _____ at _____

Health insurance: _____

Neighbour: _____ at _____

Relative: _____ at _____

Our blood types and allergies

_____ Type: _____ Allergies: _____

_____ Type: _____ Allergies: _____

Fire: _____

Police: _____

Poison centre: _____

Hospital emergency room: _____

Ambulance: _____

what to take and when is a worry of the past.

Another aid to the elderly, when it comes to pills, is helping them clear out medicine chests bulging with out-of-date pills and potions. Nothing could be more dangerous for the absent-minded.

BABYSITTER'S CHECKLIST

We often employ quite young and inexperienced people, and pay them very little, to look after the most precious things in the world – our children. No matter how you rationalise it, this is odd behaviour!

To set your mind at ease, make sure you've covered the following topics with babysitters who come to work for you.

■ What to do in case of fire, choking incident, attempted break-in or threatening telephone call.

■ Name and telephone number of a near neighbour likely to be home (preferably one experienced with children).

■ Where you will be and where you are likely to move on to.

■ The importance of taking telephone messages accurately.

■ The whereabouts of the main rooms of the house, how to lock the windows and doors, how

to turn on external lights.

■ Make sure the babysitter understands that he or she must stay with the children when they are awake and check them when they are asleep (one babysitter took two four-year-olds to a pantomime in the city, left them and went shopping until it was supposed to end!)

■ If a medicine has to be given during the time you will be out, explain this step by step, including what you suggest they do if the child spits it or vomits it back up.

■ The spelling and pronunciation of your name and address.

■ Any 'local rules' your children know about, but which they may try to break, such as 'we take a swim in the pool after dinner' or 'Mummy lets me watch TV till 10.30'.

■ Stress that they are not to open the door to strangers.

■ Children's particular quirks, so the babysitter doesn't deny a bottle of juice in bed, thereby causing a great upset and a child who cannot sleep.

Always write down your destination, telephone numbers and an alternative contact for your child's sitter to refer to. Keep this information in a prominent position where it can be easily referred to

SAFE POWER SOURCES

Adults are grateful for the many tasks that electricity and gas make easy for them, but they have also learnt to respect these potentially dangerous sources of power – unlike children.

Children need to be taught at an early age that both gas and electricity are very dangerous if tampered with.

Any home child-proofing or safety scheme must include a detailed look at both electricity and gas.

ELECTRICITY

✳ If you are in any doubt about wiring or appliance repairs, call in a qualified electrician.

✳ When disconnecting an appliance or light, first make sure your hands are dry. Switch the object off, then switch the power off at the wall and then pull the plug out, but don't pull by the cord itself. This simple ritual should always be performed without variation, particularly in front of impressionable children.

✳ A cord that is damaged in any way should be replaced, as should any cracked plugs or power points.

✳ Keep hairdryers and other portable electrical applicances out of the bathroom at all times.

✳ Heaters should never be in bathrooms either, unless they are wall-mounted.

✳ Appliance cords, except on double-insulated equipment, need to have an 'earth' wire. This will ensure that any fault will flow to earth via that wire instead of via the user's body!

✳ Touching electrical wires can kill. A tall boat mast, for instance, could strike wires when it is being put into the water. A kite could strike wires near the park. A metal ladder could hit wires connected to your eaves. Remember, 'Look up and Live'!

✳ Electric blankets, which only adults should use (and not incontinent adults), need to be tied with their tapes so that they don't crease or fold when they are on.

✳ Strong pesticides and household cleaners should not be sprayed onto power points, as they could crack.

✳ Cover power points with little plastic plugs, because small children spend a lot of their time at floor level.

✳ If the floor of your laundry is constantly getting wet, make sure you wear rubber-soled shoes when using the washing machine.

✳ Electrical mowers, trimmers and edgers should have cords out of the way when being used.

✳ Check before you dig. Underground cables may be buried where you want to dig.

✳ If fuses keep blowing, don't just keep replacing them. Have the cause of the fault put right.

✳ A common, but dangerous, practice is to stack more and more double adaptors onto the one power point. This is a very real fire hazard.

✳ A power strike or a

power failure can be dangerous if you don't turn off all the appliances you were using when the power cut out. A bar heater or a pan of food suddenly coming to life at 3 a.m. can be extremely dangerous.

❋ It is a good idea to install a residual current device (RCD). If an electrical fault develops and power flows to earth, the RCD will cut off power to prevent an otherwise fatal electrocution. This may be installed on the meter-box so that all circuits are covered or in one area only such as the kitchen where only the power points on that circuit are protected.

GAS LEAKS

Gas can leak from a gas meter, in the pipe leading from your meter to the appliance, or it can leak from the appliance itself.

An added problem these days is that most homes are connected to natural gas, therefore the nauseating tell-tale smell of leaking gas, so easy to detect 'in the old days' is no longer with us.

The simplest solution if you detect a gas leak, is to turn all gas appliances off, turn all pilot lights off, and call a qualified technician to run some tests for you.

If you would prefer to do the testing yourself, turn off all gas appliances and pilot lights and find your gas meter. Take a note of the reading and look at the red pointers. Mark its position with masking tape. Is there any visible movement while you're standing there? If so, you have a significant

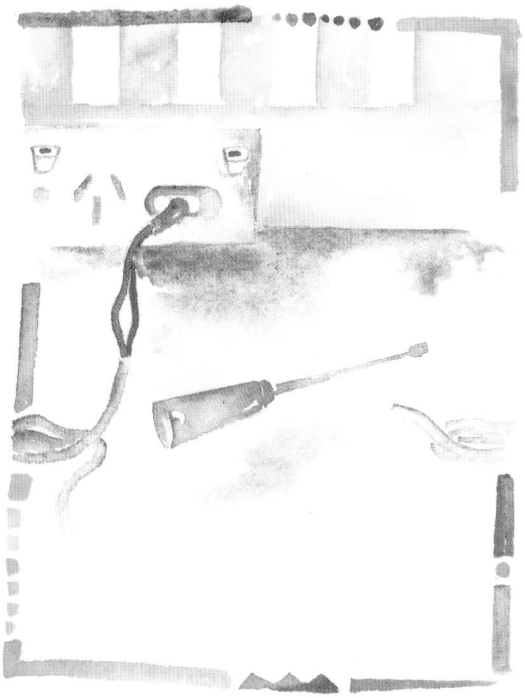

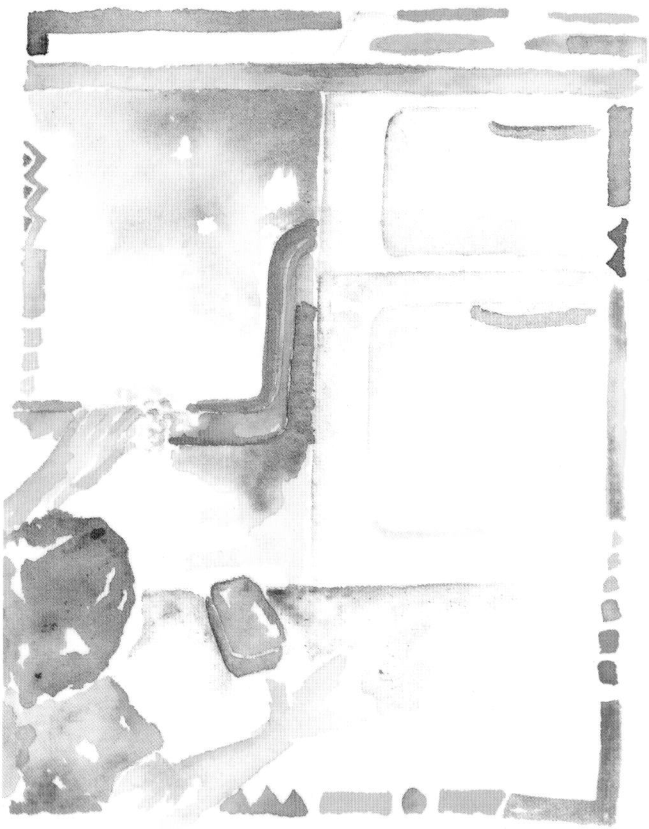

leak.

If nothing moves while you're standing there, come back after an hour (don't use any appliances in that time) and read the meter again. Has it changed? Yes? Then you can suspect a leak.

A leaking pipe can be tested by coating it in soapy water. There could be a leak if little bubbles start appearing on the pipe.

Although it sounds unbelievably obvious, it's worth repeating – don't go looking for a gas leak with the aid of a match, candle or any kind of naked flame!

Also, never let little children 'help' you relight pilot lights or light a gas oven or be anywhere nearby until they are old enough to understand.

Gas leaks are dangerous so have them looked at as soon as possible.

TIPSTRIP

- Whether you have an electric or a gas hot water system, one way of minimising the risks of hot water burns and scalds to your children in baths and showers is to get thermostatic mixing valves which can be set to a safe temperature.
- Another option is to turn down the thermostat on the water heater itself.
- Yet another option is to install child-proof taps which you have to push down with some force. As soon as the tap is released the water shuts off.
- Make sure your stove, gas or electric, is well anchored to the wall. Young children have been known to pull down the oven door and stand on it to see what's happening inside. The consequences can be horrific.

It's not just sharp knives and appalling cooking that constitute the perils of the kitchen. The modern kitchen is alive with safety problems, ranging from fire to choking!

THE KITCHEN

Heart of the home, but how safe?

The kitchen is used all day, often starting with heating a baby's bottle or making a cup of tea at dawn and going through to making a midnight snack. How safe are your daily kitchen practices?

Many accidents in the home occur in the kitchen! Make sure that all electrical cords are out of harm's way and are not dangling over kitchen worktops where they are likely to be pulled

SAFETY POINTERS

Consideration of the following safety points should help to reduce the potential hazards in the kitchen.

✳ Early in the morning, keep yourself away from boiling, scalding liquids as you are only half awake. Have respect for kettles and hotplates.

✳ Don't ever put metal forks or knives into a toaster to remove recalcitrant slices of toast. If you must delve in there, switch the power off at the wall and remove the toaster's plug.

✳ Make sure that cords are as short as possible or are curled to avoid the hazard of them dangling over the edge of worktops. Replace old and frayed cords.

✳ Keep appliances well away from the sink or any other areas where there is water.

✳ Keep cups of tea, coffee and hot soup way back on the worktop.

✳ When cooking with hot oils or fats, don't leave the kitchen. If a fire should start, do you have a fire blanket or mini-extinguisher in the kitchen? Do you know that you can extinguish a fire in a pan by putting its lid on, thereby depriving the fire of the oxygen it needs? Another quick trick is to toss a fire blanket or wet tea towel over the pan, then turn off the heat. Don't pick up the pan – you'll burn yourself badly – and don't throw water on the fire. Oven fires can also be put out by turning off the source of heat and keeping the oven closed.

✳ Steam burns are the worst, so always respect steam. To check food, lift saucepan lids away from you, and wait for steam to subside a little. Check that your kettle lid fits securely.

✳ If using matches to light ovens or hobs, light the match before turning on the gas. As an extra precaution with ovens, make sure you open the oven door to let any accumulated gas escape before lighting a match or pressing the automatic oven lighting button.

✳ The kitchen floor should have a slip-resistant surface.

✳ Turn saucepan handles inwards, towards the back of the stove, away from grabbing little persons who want to 'help' with the cooking, but don't position the handles over another lit hob, whatever you do.

✳ Using a damp tea towel to lift hot dishes from the oven can result in severe scalds. Keep proper oven mitts close at hand.

✳ Secure storage of sharp knives and other potentially dangerous utensils is a must. See further on in this section for our Storing Sharp Utensils project.

✳ Make sure that the lids on rubbish bins are securely sealed.

✳ Under the kitchen sink is usually an Aladdin's Cave for children. As most of the caustic and highly poisonous liquids and powders are kept under

The electric jug should be unplugged when not in use. Two child-safe features have been installed. Firstly, the power point features a safety shutter switch which cuts off automatically if a foreign object is put in the socket. The left-hand power point has a plastic cover protecting enquiring hands from danger

Keep potentially dangerous items, such as detergents and cleaning agents, out of a child's reach with an easily installed child-proof safety latch

35

the sink, child-proofing this cupboard is a must. See page 42 for our project on child-resistant cupboard catches.

✳ Dishwashing powders and liquids for automatic dishwashers are capable of burning a young throat if drunk. Lock these away with other household poisons, and support those manufacturers who put their dishwashing powder or liquid in child-proof containers.

✳ Old plastic soft drink bottles or any recognisable food containers will, to a child's way of thinking, still contain that yummy drink or food, no matter what's really in them now. Never store poisonous liquids or powders in anything other than the bottle, jar or container they came in, even if these plastic containers are usually in places where children do not normally play, like tool sheds.

✳ Keep some child-proof containers after they're empty (for example, a child-proof plastic bottle of automatic dishwashing liquid) so that you can safely store the contents of a broken bottle, but be sure to relabel it clearly.

✳ Keep hands dry around electrical appliances and around switches, particularly waste disposal switches near the sink. Speaking of 'garbage munchers', never try to unblock one while it's going. Switch it off, then wait a few seconds before putting your hand in.

✳ Aprons with large pockets can be a problem if the pocket catches on saucepan handles or on cupboard door knobs. Keep this in mind when buying your next apron.

✳ Can your kitchen's wiring cope with the next influx of appliances after Mother's Day, Father's Day, Christmas or birthday?

✳ Before you pick up anything hot, make space on the worktop for putting it down.

✳ Before putting a new blade or attachment onto a food processor, turn it off at the switch. For extra safety, unplug the machine.

✳ Sharp knives can slip when held in greasy or wet hands. Clean and dry your hands before using them, and don't ever cut towards your body.

✳ Thirty or so years ago appliances such as the dishwasher, microwave, clothes dryer and video were rare and therefore there were less demands on the wiring. If your home has old wiring check that it is able to handle the demands of modern day appliances.

ENERGY RATING OF YOUR APPLIANCES

A handy guide to the power consumption of the typical household appliances found in the home:

Clothes dryer	2400 Watts
Dishwasher	2400 Watts
Electric jug	1800 Watts
Hairdryer	2400 Watts
Iron	1000 Watts
Lights	300 Watts
Microwave	1350 Watts
Television/video	240 Watts
Washing machine (non-heating)	600 Watts

Children at an early age need to be taught that the oven is very dangerous. Keep saucepan handles turned inward when cooking but away from other elements. The easy installation of an oven top railing provides extra safety

KEEP FOOD SAFE

Food safety is an important consideration. It is important with respect to babies and there are also hazards that the elderly, if living on their own, should be aware of.

Dehydration from gastric problems can be very serious for young babies.

Similarly, elderly people are less resilient than younger people and their food therefore needs to be prepared and stored with great care.

When choosing, buying or preparing the food, here are some general tips to think about:

✳ The frozen food aisle should be your last port of call in the supermarket. You will notice it is often the last aisle anyway. Take frozen purchases home straight away and put them in the freezer.

✳ If, for whatever reason, the food has thawed before you get a chance to get it into a freezer, the sad truth is that it should be cooked and eaten that day or thrown out – never refrozen.

✳ Frozen poultry should never be cooked half-thawed. Thaw fully before cooking it (refer to our chart on defrosting). Chopping boards and knives used in cutting thawed poultry should be kept away from other foods.

✳ Never use damaged cans of food.

✳ Before starting any cooking, wash your hands with soap, dry them well, tie long hair back, put on an apron and try to cook in the way that you'd hope professionals or restauranteurs would cook! Avoid licking spoons and putting them back into the mixture, or tasting soups and then putting the ladle back in.

✳ Clean up as you go, taking particular care to put milk and other dairy products back into the fridge as soon as you've finished with them. Even five minutes sitting in a warm kitchen can make milk 'go off' quickly.

✳ Leftovers should be refrigerated as soon as possible. Cover them properly with plastic wrap or foil.

✳ Be scrupulously careful with washing up, especially if someone in your home already has a gastric problem. Boil their eating utensils, or pour boiling water over them, to prevent any bugs spreading to other family members.

Always check the Use-by date of pre-packed purchased food, especially meat-based products. These foods lose their freshness quickly if not stored properly or eaten promptly. Over-stocking of these goods at home, combined with poor storage, is a definite health hazard

DEFROST WITH CONFIDENCE (microwave)

TYPE	TIME USING DEFROST SETTING*	INSTRUCTIONS
Whole white fish or fillets	3 to 4 minutes per 500 g	Turn fish half way through defrosting, stand 10 minutes
Whole chicken	6 to 8 minutes per 500 g	Turn half way through defrosting.
Chicken pieces	5 to 7 minutes per 500 g	Separate and rearrange during defrosting
Steaks	8 to 10 minutes per 500 g	Turn over half way through defrosting
Sausages	5 to 6 minutes per 500 g	Separate and rearrange half way through defrosting

* These are times for a 700 watt microwave oven. Increase defrost times for 500 watt microwave ovens by about 10%

Sharp knives, and other sharp utensils used in the kitchen are too often simply stored in a drawer which is easily accessible to small, inquisitive fingers.

Project 8

Storing Sharp Utensils

Sharp utensils should be stored above the reach of children, preferably in a cupboard with a safety catch. One simple method is to fix a rack to the wall above the workbench or to the inside of a cupboard door.

The rack presented in this project is simple to make or can be bought ready-made from hardware stores.

There are many other alternative methods of storing knives which may include plastic coated steel mesh wall panels. These panels are screwed to the wall with hooks for hanging knives and other utensils.

Prefabricated timber knife racks with a magnetic metal strip are also very common at hardware stores and are a very convenient way of storing knives out of the way.

STEP BY STEP

1 Decide on the length of the knife rack. You should allow approximately 50 mm for each knife.

2 Use a tenon saw or fine toothed panel saw to cut the timber to length.

3 Use a small block plane to plane down the edges or use fine sandpaper to level all the edges.

4 Cut two lengths of 6 mm thick timber, or plywood, for packing at each end. Glue these to the timber strip with PVA adhesive.

5 When the adhesive is dried, sand down the whole unit, drive a hole at each end for screw fixing to the wall. These holes should be countersunk.

6 Mark the location of the rack on the wall by using a spirit level to find the level position.

7 Drill holes for wall fixings. For masonry walls use 6 mm diameter screws set into rawl plugs. Plasterboard lined walls will require toggle bolts.

WHAT TO BUY
☐ 40 mm x 12 mm planed timber, length to suit, 6 mm thick
☐ brass wood screws if fixing to timber or masonry, zinc-plated toggle bolts for plasterboard walls
☐ PVA adhesive (glue)

TOOLS
☐ tenon saw/fine toothed panel saw
☐ drill
☐ small block plane
☐ spirit level

TIME
Approximately 2 hours

12 6

40

BEVEL ALL EDGES OF THE TIMBER WITH A SANDING BLOCK

WHEN COMPLETE FINISH OFF WITH TWO COATS OF CLEAR POLYURETHANE

KNIFE RACK FOR FIXING TO THE WALL ABOVE THE BENCH OR INSIDE A CUPBOARD

250

18

THIS IS A SUGGESTED LENGTH WHICH SHOULD BE DETERMINED TO SUIT YOUR LOCATION

DO   **DON'T**

The way to do it!

Don't load your cutlery container this way – hasty or careless container removal, or simply the stacking of plates, can lead to dangerous collisions with those knife points and nasty cuts

KITCHEN SAFETY FOR THE ELDERLY

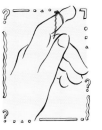

Nowadays there are many companies that cater for the elderly with various kitchen gadgets. Many supply catalogues listing these.

■ Don't take risks with boiling liquids. Only heat a sufficient amount for your immediate needs.

■ When cooking vegetables, use a wire mesh cooking basket which can be lifted out from the pan, leaving the boiling water in the pan to cool.

■ A timer tucked into your pocket can be set to ring when your vegetables are ready. That way you will avoid both ruined pans and a ruined meal.

■ Make sure there is a heat-proof surface beside the sink and the cooker so you can set down hot and heavy cookware.

■ Use anything from children's plasticine or play dough to beads and self-adhesive tags, to highlight the OFF position on the dials of your gas or electric cooker.

■ Ensure that there is adequate lighting and non-slip surfaces in your kitchen. Never place loose rugs or matting on a kitchen floor.

■ Arrange items used everyday, like bread, milk, tea or coffee, within easy reach to cut down on stooping, stretching and possible spillages.

The bathroom is one dangerous place with a variety of built-in hazards – water mixing with electricity, soapy tiles, slippery surfaces and the fact that most medicines are stored in there.

THE BATHROOM

Small, but oh how important!

Many accidents in the home take place in the bathroom. People persist in having heaters, radios and hairdryers near showers and baths.

It is a common mistake to continue to keep and store old medicines, long past their Use-by date, either through laziness, forgetfulness or under the mistaken impression that if they get a certain condition again, the remains of the medicine used to treat it this time round will still be fine.

Most medicines should be stored in a cool, dry place. Bathroom cabinets are particularly unsuitable since they are warm and humid!

Many accidents occur in the bathroom as the surfaces are both slippery and hard. It is a good idea to install grip rails and non-slip mats.

Have a look at our guidelines for bathroom safety.

The bathroom is an area that demands strict supervision. Replace the hot tap faucet with a childproof safety tap that requires the hot tap to be pressed in first before it will turn

DO

■ Do take special care in running a baby's bath. Put in cold water first, hot water next and then run some cold water again to cool down the tap itself.

■ Do install grip rails to help elderly relatives as well as young children who may need something secure to hold onto in baths and showers.

■ Do buy non-slip mats for use in the shower, the bath and on the bathroom floor.

■ Do teach children never to run into the bathroom and teach them to wipe up wet floors after themselves.

■ Do install a privy lock which allows the door to be unlocked from the outside.

■ Do install a thermostatic mixing valve which pre-sets the water at a safe temperature (that is not scalding hot).

■ Do install a child-proof safety tap that prevents toddler's hands from turning on the hot tap.

■ Do use covers and other obstacles as they were meant to be used, for example, make it a habit to put the lid down on the toilet so that curious little ones don't explore in there or fall in.

■ Do fill the bath with cold water first, then the hot water or use the mixer tap.

■ Do avoid sharp corners when planning a new bathroom.

DON'T

■ Don't use electric heaters of any kind (unless wall mounted, with an insulated cord) or electrically powered radios, telephones, hair dryers, electric shavers or *anything* electrically powered in the bathroom, other than properly installed lights and properly insulated towel warming rails.

■ Don't keep old medicines – return them to a pharmacy for safe disposal. Current medicines should be safely stored out of harm's way.

■ Don't leave any child under the age of about six in the bath alone. Extend the age if you have particularly boisterous or accident-prone children. If you feel you can trust your over-fours, at least stay within earshot if you're not going to stay in the bathroom with them.

■ Don't keep antiseptic solutions, toilet bowl cleaners and so on in the bathroom unless securely locked up. These are usually highly caustic.

■ Don't ever leave a baby in a bath alone. A baby can drown in just a few centimetres of water. If the phone or doorbell rings or other children call for you, ignore them. If ignoring them's not possible, scoop the half-bathed baby up in a towel and take it with you.

■ Don't leave sharp implements such as razors in accessible places. Make sure that used razor blades are wrapped up and placed in outdoor rubbish bins.

■ Don't install extra deep baths as they present a danger to the young toddler. The closer the bath's rim to the floor, the more easily a child can climb it and fall in.

■ Don't position the towel bars anywhere where they may be used as a handrail by a climbing toddler.

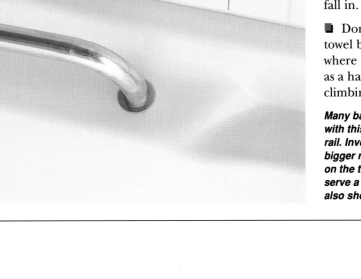

Many baths are now fitted with this convenient safety rail. Investigate installing a bigger rail slightly higher up on the tiled wall which will serve a dual purpose if you also shower in your bath

Any household with small children should have at least one cupboard fitted with a safety catch for the storage of dangerous liquids, medicines and poisons.

Project 9

Child-resistant Catches

A number of safety catches are available from hardware stores. One such inexpensive catch is illustrated in our project.

P ills that look and taste like sweets are attractive but very dangerous to young children. It is important to go through all bathroom and kitchen drawers and cabinets.

Take out all cleansers, medicines, cosmetics, household detergents and sharp objects, and any other potential poisons.

Store these in drawers or cupboards fitted with this safety catch, that is available from most hardware shops. This will keep curious young children out of cupboards that house dangerous items.

WHAT TO BUY

TOOLS
☐ electric or hand drill

TIME
Approximately half an hour

SLOTTED CATCH SCREWED TO UNDERSIDE OF CUPBOARD OR DRAWER FRAME

SHAFT SCREWED TO DOOR OR DRAWER FRONT POINTING UPWARDS SO THAT IT ALIGNS WITH CATCH

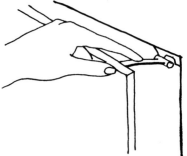

SAFETY CATCH RELEASED BY OPENING DRAWER OR CUPBOARD AND DEPRESSING THE SHAFT

SHAFT UNIT FIXED TO INSIDE OF DOOR OR DRAWER. SLOTTED HOLES ALLOW FOR HEIGHT ADJUSTMENT

TIPSTRIP

■ Do elderly relatives lock up their pills, or are these kept at bedside tables and in other accessible places? Have a word with them about this before your little ones visit or stay overnight.

■ There are locks available these days that can be opened from either side of the door. These are invaluable in those cases where a young child has locked him or herself in the bathroom.

The tough plastic shaft is screwed to the inside of the door and clips into a slotted catch on the underside of the cupboard when the door is closed.

When the door is opened there is enough room available for an adult's finger to push the shaft down to disengage the catch from the slotted part, making it easy for mum or dad to open but impossible for smaller children.

Any existing cupboard door or drawer in the kitchen, bathroom or even the tool shed can be easily fitted with this type of child-proof catch. Remember that just-crawling or just-walking toddlers will get into almost any conceivable nook or cranny. Having a safety catch on specific cupboards means peace of mind.

STEP BY STEP

1 Mark the position for the slotted catch and shaft. The hardware suppliers that carry these safety catches will probably be able to suggest the correct distance from the door edge.

2 Screw fix the slotted catch to the underside of the cupboard. Follow the supplier's instructions for the exact position.

3 Screw fix the shaft to the inside edge of the door. This unit has slotted holes for fine adjustment in a vertical position.

4 Adjust the shaft so that it falls easily into the slotted catch when the door closes.

SHOWER SEAT AND GRAB RAIL

Climbing in and out of slippery baths and showers can be hazardous for both the young and the old. It's made much safer when there are strategically placed bars to grab hold of.

Safety rails are available from hardware suppliers in kit form. These kits will usually include fixing screws and bolts for masonry and hollow walls. Make sure the fixing coincides with studs and noggings if the wall is hollow.

Accessories, such as removable seats for showers are optional. These types of rails should be considered for inclusion in bathrooms used by elderly residents and those not too steady on their legs.

Above: For safety in the bathroom install a shower seat and grab rail

GRAB RAILS

REMOVABLE HANGING SEAT

43

Safety and security are top priorities when planning your child's room. Always remember anything that can go wrong, will go wrong. Anticipate the potential dangers and use your common sense to prevent accidents.

MODERN BEDROOMS
Today's bedroom is a multipurpose room

Your child's bedroom is one of the few places where you won't always be able to keep a watchful eye over them. Because of this, it's important to eliminate any potential sources of danger before small children are left on their own.

Ensure that the doors to the rooms of older brothers and sisters stay closed to the adventurous toddler. Carefully check wooden furniture for any sign of splitting. Bunks are best left to older children

Storage chests present a real danger to children's fingers if the lid falls shut and crushes them. A stopper should be fitted to allow a sufficient gap when the chest is fully closed

There are some obvious problem areas in the bedroom which apply equally for all rooms in the home.

CHILD-FRIENDLY POINTERS

❋ Inspect all bedrooms for hazards such as throw rugs, which are dangerous as small children can slip on them easily.

❋ Bunks or beds for small children should be fitted with safety rails and they should not be allowed to sleep in the top bunk.

❋ Furniture should have rounded edges where possible and be very stable. Ensure extra stability by buying chunky kid-sized pieces.

❋ Electrical fittings should be shielded or located out of harm's way. Fit unused power points with safety socket covers.

❋ An overhead light, with a dimmer switch, is probably a better idea than a night light, which is pretty sure to be knocked over and possibly broken. Try to have a light switch that the toddler can reach, such as a pull-cord light.

❋ When a toddler gets to the toilet training stage, encourage this as much as possible by making sure each night there is a clear, stumble-free path to the bathroom. You might also consider leaving the bathroom light on all

night for a few months, for extra encouragement and safety. A toddler who's given a toy torch which works, will make extra efforts to be toilet trained, and will be safer too. Get one that switches itself off after a few minutes!

❋ Carpet is the friendliest choice for children's bedrooms. Treat the carpet with a stain repellent so that spills will be easier to wipe up.

When considering new furniture opt for sturdiness, rounded edges and stability

TOYS – KEEPING PLAYTIME SAFE

Children of all ages love to play and this should be encouraged. It is during playtime that children explore and discover their environment. Through toys, children learn to manipulate objects, test things out and find out how objects work.

✻ Always choose toys for your children which are suitable for their age group. Toys which are safe for one child may be highly unsuitable for another.

✻ Regularly check to see if little pieces of toys or other gear have broken off, leaving a sharp edge. Be ruthless about tossing things out.

✻ Consumer guides to toys which are safe, and which children really like, are invaluable. Look for some of these guides in your local library.

✻ Don't give babies or toddlers toys which are too advanced for them. Be careful to keep older brothers' and sisters' toys out of reach, and when buying new toys, read the labels for the manufacturer's age recommendation.

✻ Rattles and any noise-making toys should always be viewed with a jaundiced eye. Could the toy break and the noise-making bits fall out and be swallowed? Also look at the eyes of stuffed animals and dolls with care. Try very hard to

pull them off. If they can't be budged, they are probably OK, for the time being. After a little chewing and manipulating they may not be safe any more.

✻ Check that any plastic toys are of firm though bendable plastic which will not shatter causing sharp splinters if broken.

✻ Babies love balloons but torn balloon bits can choke them. Be careful after older children's parties that all balloon debris is thrown out.

✻ Try to insist that tricycles, block trolleys, mini skateboards and all other toys with wheels are stored outside. At the top of a flight of stairs, or in a badly lit child's room, they can be lethal.

✻ Toy boxes, while often looking beautiful, are not safe unless they have a spring built into the lid that stops it from banging down on the inevitably curious toddler.

When it is shut, there must be air holes, preferably up near the top of the box because toys at the bottom of the box will cover any air holes down there. Toy boxes really are better for older children, who can rummage around more easily and know about putting things back. Little ones would be just as happy with some low shelves or brightly covered cardboard boxes.

✻ You should be careful with noise-producing toys since they may actually be too loud for the children who play with them and could damage their hearing. For a child of less than 18 months, 'continuous' noise should be no more than 75 decibels and 'impulsive' noise should be no more than 105 decibels.

✻ Liquid-filled imported toys should be checked for labels stating that the liquid they contain is not harmful or contaminated in any way, should the child break or bite the toy and release the liquid. If such a label is not included, do not buy the toy.

✳ Train them not to snap back masks and helmets held by elastic. Serious injuries occur in this way. The mask or helmet should also be well ventilated if it is made of plastic or metal.

✳ A trampoline, especially if more than one child climbs on it, is very dangerous. Leave trampolines in the circus or in the gymnasium, where they belong and where expert, constant supervision is the order of the day. Little rebounders, on the other hand, are great fun for small children, and are relatively safe.

In summary, the right toys are an invaluable way of

RESTFUL ROOMS

For most of us, the bedroom is a haven of quiet and rest, but havoc can be wreaked there just as easily as in many other rooms of the average house! Follow our safety pointers:

◻ Smoking in bed, even when you are sitting up and feeling 100 per cent awake, is a very unsafe practice. (Smoking full stop is a very unsafe practice, but that's another story!)

◻ Keep any bar heaters clear of bedclothes that may be tossed off during the night. Preferably, use radiators or any other heating without direct flame or element to heat bedrooms.

◻ Children should never have electric blankets. Do not consider them until your children are in their teens and way past any possibility of even an isolated case of bed-wetting. By the same token, incontinent adults should not have electric blankets either. Have your electric blanket checked regularly; when taking out of storage and before each winter season.

◻ Stumbling around a bedroom can be dangerous for both children and the elderly, so make sure there is a source of background light somewhere in the bedroom or just outside the door.

◻ An adult's dressing table attracts small children like a magnet, so be aware of the substances it might have on top. There may be nail polish and nail polish remover, hair-spray, cosmetics, perfume, vitamins or even prescription medication for ease of access, but dangerous in the hands of youngsters.

◻ For a long time now, parents have been aware of the need to buy flame resistant, non-flowing nightwear for young children. Do the same for elderly relatives too.

amusing and stimulating your child, as well as developing his or her co-ordination skills. Things to consider when buying toys are:

✳ Will constant parental supervision be necessary?

✳ Will maintenance of the toy be required?

✳ Can the toy be used safely anywhere?

For children of two years and older, a doll's house can provide hours of safe initiative play. Do make sure that older children's possessions are kept away from younger siblings

TIPSTRIP

■ Never leave a bottle propped up in a baby's mouth. The baby could easily choke.

■ Don't drink hot tea, coffee or soups when holding or feeding a baby.

■ Don't carry saucepans of hot liquids or hot drinks near a crawling baby. You are almost certain to trip.

■ Never put bouncers on table tops - easy for you to keep the bouncing motion going, but even easier for a baby to slowly but surely bounce himself off the edge of the table.

■ When putting your baby to bed, make sure that you have removed the bib.

Once baby arrives the nursery will be used extensively. The baby's room requires special forethought and safety features should be looked at in great detail, from the selection of furniture through to the toys and mobiles.

BABY'S NURSERY
Planning a baby-proof environment

SAFETY POINTERS

The baby's nursery can be very streamlined and plain, it can be very colourful, or it can be over the top with lots of frills and bows. One factor that is consistent with all nurseries is that of safety.

Follow these guidelines to help make your baby's nursery safer.

❋ Old, unrenovated houses may well have lead-based paint on the walls and ceilings. Ditto old, hand-me-down prams or cots. Strip back and repaint.

❋ The amount of space between cot bars and between the mattress and cot sides should be such that no body parts can wedge between them.

❋ Hand-me-down cots with drop sides can be very dangerous if the catch holding up the sides is loose after many years of use. Make sure the side will stay up securely until

The time before the arrival of a new baby is the perfect time to prepare a new nursery

an adult chooses to release it. The latch should be slightly difficult to do.

✱ The baby who couldn't roll over yesterday will learn to do it today, either while on your bed or on the changing table. In the first instance, the baby may well fall. In the second, the changing table **should** have slightly raised sides and a safety strap, which is a bore to use every time you change the baby, but which is really very necessary. A fall from a changing table is usually worse than one from a bed, as the table is much higher.

✱ Keep talcum powder away from baby as it has a very real danger of obstructing air passages if breathed in.

✱ Always take the bib off before putting baby to bed as he or she could choke.

✱ Cut-outs in cot headboards may look very cute, but are they big enough for a part of the baby's body to become wedged?

✱ Toys strung across cots are fine until the baby shows signs of head-lifting. They should then be removed and strung across the buggy.

✱ Things you'd never think of as being hazards, like pretty ribbons hanging from a cot toy, or the cord of a toy phone should not be anywhere near a baby.

✱ Check the baby's dummy has no loose bits

and replace it before it falls apart.

✱ Babies don't need pillows (the risk of

suffocation is too great) and they need mattresses which breathe, especially in the early weeks of life.

BABY CHECKLIST

◘ Are power points at skirting board level covered?

◘ Anything small on the floor? You can be sure it will be picked up and inserted in the mouth.

◘ Is your nappy bucket tightly lidded? Babies can actually drown in them. It is sensible to keep the nappy bucket in the laundry. Are any deodorising or sterilising chemicals out of reach?

◘ How about loose cords?

Tie them up out of the way, including blind cords, or clip them down if they are electrical cords.

◘ Beware of buttons on babies' clothes and of any hooks or handles around the room. Babies can get themselves tangled up, sometimes seriously, on the most unlikely things.

◘ Check that there is no way the baby can crawl up to an open window, and out. During these dangerous early years, it might be worth fixing the window with a bolt or heavy pin.

◘ Can your baby climb out of its cot? If so, he or she is ready for a bed, with or without a roll bar.

◘ Never leave your baby

on the changing table unattended. Make sure the changing table is sturdy and that it has secure side rails.

◘ Have everything you need for the changing table in handy reach. Store

all your baby's powders, creams and nappies under the changing table and out of your baby's reach.

◘ Make sure all the toys in your baby's nursery are large and soft with no small removable parts.

The days when children were seen and not heard are long gone. There are rarely going to be any areas in a house where children are forbidden entry. So it's vital to remember to keep all general areas in a house safe and secure, including hallways, living rooms and so on.

LIVING AREAS

Where accidents can happen, and do

The family room and lounge area, and all of those in-between nooks and crannies, are important safety priorities. These are the areas where all the family relaxes and has fun – make them extra safe.

Nowadays, a strong feature of every home is a space where all the family can feel comfortable together. In fact, many people refer to this space as the family room, living room or lounge.

In it, you find any combination of television, video recorder, stereo and/or compact disc, comfortable chairs, book shelves, rugs, board games, toys, small tables and a respectable amount of mess!

All the electrical appliances in general family areas should have good air circulation around them. They are likely to get a lot of use and must be able to cool themselves down.

Heating the family areas safely should be a major concern too. Rugs, bean bags, cushions and other materials that could combust should be kept clear of any heating devices. Adequate built-in heaters are an important safety feature and such systems should be installed by a professional. With all heaters, make sure that

the element is inaccessible to young children. It is a good idea to install a smoke detector in the family room.

An open fire is very pleasant but is particularly dangerous. Younger children should never be left without adult supervision in a room with an open fire. While the children are young it is wise not to use the fireplace until they can appreciate the potential danger. If there is a fireplace, a large sturdy screen should be firmly attached. It is a good idea to keep fireplace tongs and other tools out of reach. Chimneys should be cleaned when winter is over.

Make careful choices when buying children's nightwear. Avoid long, baggy or frilly nightwear. Choose nightwear that is close fitting and made from flame-resistant materials.

Chairs and couches in these living areas should

be well padded and tables should have rounded edges and corners so that they are friendlier for younger children.

Ensure that the furniture has been upholstered with flame-

resistant finishings and fabrics.

All light fixtures need to be placed high on the walls and all free-standing lamps, as they are easily knocked over, should be eliminated.

To be safe, make sure that all indoor pot plants are well out of the reach of the adventurous toddler. Check that the plants you have are not poisonous.

OFFICE AND STUDY AREAS

Most home offices are corners of other rooms, snatched by whichever partner is faster on his/her feet! But many can present traps: everything from swallowed paper clips to a computer monitor pulled onto a small head – it's all possible.

These spaces that have been set aside for specialised work, such as the home office and sewing room, are not usually designed with children in mind. Such areas require locks either on doors or on cabinets to lock away dangerous items.

Computers need to be out of reach otherwise you may find your toddler chewing on a floppy disk containing invaluable notes, such as the year's tax information!

Equipment and supplies in an office could typically include the following:
☐ typewriter
☐ copier
☐ facsimile
☐ phone/answerphone
☐ filing cabinet
☐ safe
☐ copier chemicals
☐ typewriter ribbons
☐ floppy disks

Make sure that all equipment of this sort is installed safely.

When installing computers and facsimile machines make sure that there is adequate and sturdy shelving for disks and stationery. Make sure that there is good lighting.

A rolltop desk allows for working space and provides adequate lockable storage for items, such as pencils, paper, clips and rubberbands that are dangerous in the hands of toddlers.

Keep children out of the home office. It is important that they understand that it is a work place and not a playroom.

HOBBY AREAS

As children reach the ages of ten and twelve they become keen hobbyists, be it computers, model planes or simply listening to music. Such hobbies require planned space. As children will spend a lot of time in this designated area, a sturdy desk with adequate shelving needs to be installed. A walk-in wardrobe serves this purpose well and can be easily renovated to allow room for a working table. This work space means that the whole area can be closed off when not in use.

FRIENDLIER SURFACES

Wall and floor coverings need to be durable and easy to clean with youngsters around. Crayons, food and juice have a habit of finding their way on walls. Vinyl-coated wallpaper, plastic coverings and paint are child-friendly choices. Use non-toxic and water-based acrylic.

In many areas of the house the use of carpet is a sensible choice as is non-

Make sure that your furniture is child-friendly. Choose upholstery fabrics in patterns and colours that are not likely to show up stains easily and can be subjected to enormous amounts of wear and tear. Look for furniture that has rounded edges and corners

slip or semi-glazed floor tiles. All carpet should be treated with stain repellent so that spills can be easily wiped up. When deciding on colour for the carpet choose a medium range – one that is not too dark or too light. If the carpet is too light, stains will be highlighted and made obvious and if the carpet is too dark it can serve as a camouflage to small, sharp objects. Carpets should be regularly cleaned and vacuumed.

Bookshelves are always in demand for extra storage – they are versatile, often easily adjusted and, if secured properly, do not pose a safety problem for toddlers.

Securing Bookshelves

Bookshelf units can be dangerous when loaded up with books and magazines. This is particularly the case when children are likely to climb up to get something on the top shelf.

The same can apply to prefabricated wardrobe units.

The project shown here is a simple way of fixing a bookshelf or wardrobe to a wall.

STEP BY STEP

1 The planed timber batten is first nailed to the back of the unit.

2 Push the unit against the wall in the location required and drill through the back of the unit and through the batten into the wall. If the wall is brick, use masonry anchors for fixing. If it is a timber-stud wall, locate the studs, perhaps with the help of a stud detector, and screw direct into these.

This simple method of fixing a bookshelf unit to a wall can be used in any part of the house where children may find it necessary to climb all over it.

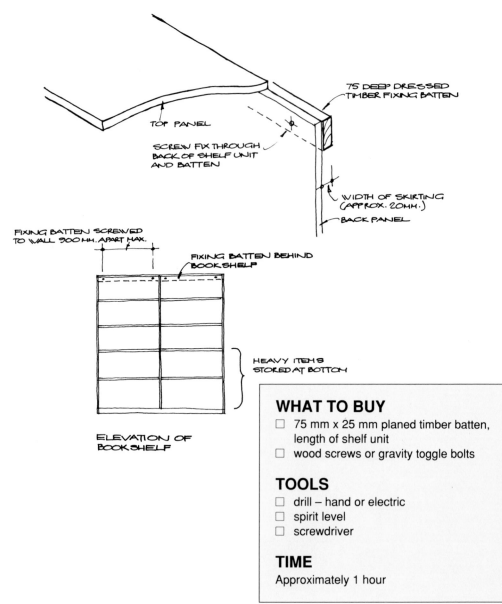

TOP PANEL

75 DEEP DRESSED TIMBER FIXING BATTEN

SCREW FIX THROUGH BACK OF SHELF UNIT AND BATTEN

WIDTH OF SKIRTING (APPROX. 20MM.)

BACK PANEL

FIXING BATTEN SCREWED TO WALL 900 MM. APART MAX.

FIXING BATTEN BEHIND BOOKSHELF

HEAVY ITEMS STORED AT BOTTOM

ELEVATION OF BOOKSHELF

WHAT TO BUY
☐ 75 mm x 25 mm planed timber batten, length of shelf unit
☐ wood screws or gravity toggle bolts

TOOLS
☐ drill – hand or electric
☐ spirit level
☐ screwdriver

TIME
Approximately 1 hour

CHILD-PROOFING

The best time to start thinking about child-proofing a home is before Child Number 1 has taken Step Number 1!

Be prepared with our child-proofing pointers. Even before your children have started to crawl, child-proof your home, because you will have precious little chance to do so afterwards!

✳ Playpens are safe, secure and give everybody 'Time Out' for a breather. They are the safest place a baby can be when somebody is ironing, for instance.

✳ Precious objects that definitely will not bounce need to be hidden and locked away. 'Out of sight, out of the rubbish bin'.

✳ Dangling tablecloths are just waiting to be pulled by a baby trying to get to its feet. Take care or over will go the glassware, cups, knives – the lot, and baby may end up bearing the brunt.

✳ Unused power points should have plastic covers inserted.

✳ Pad sharp corners of your furniture, like the corners of low coffee tables.

✳ Restraining straps in buggies, high chairs, bouncers, car seats and so on should always be used, even if the baby is only going to be there for half a minute. A lot can happen in a short time!

✳ Babies will usually climb anything in their path so make sure falls will be minor, or remove climbable objects.

✳ All accessible glass should be laminated, or else put some shatterproof film over existing glass.

✳ Try to ensure that stairs are carpeted or have some kind of non-slip cover or surface. Ditto for other floor surfaces, where possible. Rugs which are not 'anchored' in some way could result in disaster.

✳ Open fireplaces must have fireguards that are very thoroughly secured and won't tip over. They should have three sides.

✳ Outdoor railings often end several centimetres from the ground. If it is possible for your toddler to actually crawl under the base of the railing, you'll need to string up some chicken wire or something similar until they are too big to fit under any more.

✳ Windows can be made safer by putting on vertical bars, putting up secondary double-glazing panels or by installing a bolt so that it can only be opened a little way. Never fit horizontal bars – they can be climbed like a ladder.

✳ Make sure that any small or potentially unsafe object that your young child could reach and put into his or her mouth is picked up and put safely away.

✳ In areas such as hallways and stairs install three-way light switches so that the lights may be turned on or off from either end of the hallway or stairs. Alternatively plug in an inexpensive night light into a nearby outlet.

✳ Remember the iron in the laundry is hot and heavy and is best unplugged and put away when finished with. If possible have a built-in closet area for the iron and ironing board.

A toddler, curious to know how to get down a flight of stairs, can be taught with time and patience. When you're not on the spot, however, a safety gate will effectively stop the way.

Project 11

Child-safety Gate

This simple gate, designed for keeping small children away from stairs or inside rooms, can be easily made. Alternatively, a similar type of gate is available to buy.

Our gate consists of timber dowels set into a timber frame. The completed gate is slipped between timber battens screwed to the wall or door frame.

Hallways and corridors, especially at the tops of stairs, should be well lit and unobstructed by little Freddie's skateboard or building blocks. But there's an obstruction that's a must when a toddler or crawling baby is around, and that's a safety gate at the top and often at the bottom of the stairs. Make sure you have a snug fit for this vital piece of equipment.

STEP BY STEP

1 Start by cutting the top and bottom rails to the same length. Next, set out the centre of each dowel, equally divided along the length of the rails to leave a maximum separation of 50 mm between adjacent dowels. This is best done by clamping both rails together and marking the position of the dowels with a square across both rails. In this way, the dowels are all correctly aligned.

2 Cut one dowel to the correct length and then use that as a template for cutting the remainder. Glue all the dowels into the top and bottom rails with PVA adhesive and lightly clamp together, using two sash cramps. These can be hired if you don't have any. Once the cramps are in position, check that the dowels are

perpendicular to the rails with a square.

3 When the adhesive is dry – allow approximately four hours – cut the two side rails to match the height of the frame. These are fixed to the top and bottom rails by means of dowelling through the side rails into the top and bottom rails. Lightly clamp the side rails just down from the top and bottom rails. Use a dowelling drill bit which is slightly larger than the diameter of the dowels.

4 Cut the dowels to length so that they are about 10 mm longer than the depth of the hole. Squirt some adhesive into the holes and carefully hammer the dowels into the holes with a wooden mallet, leaving about 10 mm sticking out. When the adhesive is set, saw off the remainder of the dowels with a tenon saw.

5 All that remains is to take off the sharp edges with sandpaper and paint the gate with a clear polyurethane sealer to protect it from stains.

6 Timber battens to hold the gate can now be fixed in the locations you require, for

example, at the child's bedroom door or at the top of stairs or at the kitchen door to keep the child out.

WHAT TO BUY
- ☐ 2 of 50 mm x 25 mm planed rails x 2.1 m long
- ☐ 2 of 38 mm x 25 mm planed wall battens x 1.8 m long
- ☐ 6 of 12 mm diameter dowels x 1.8 m long
- ☐ 6 mm dowels x 1 m long per length
- ☐ PVA adhesive (glue)

TOOLS
- ☐ dowelling bit for 6 mm dowels
- ☐ dowelling bit for 12 mm dowels
- ☐ 2 sash cramps
- ☐ tenon saw
- ☐ electric drill and stand

TIME
4-6 hours including drying time for adhesive

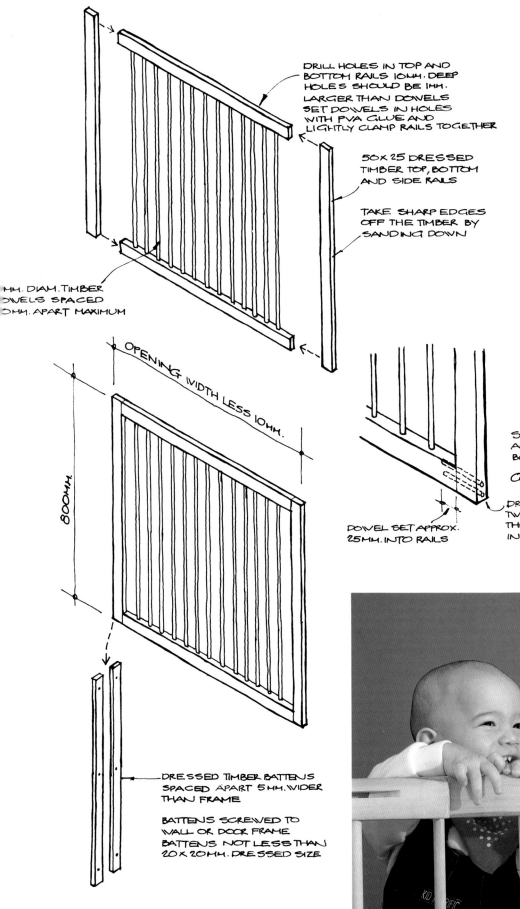

DRILL HOLES IN TOP AND BOTTOM RAILS 10MM. DEEP HOLES SHOULD BE 1MM. LARGER THAN DOWELS SET DOWELS IN HOLES WITH PVA GLUE AND LIGHTLY CLAMP RAILS TOGETHER

50 x 25 DRESSED TIMBER TOP, BOTTOM AND SIDE RAILS

TAKE SHARP EDGES OFF THE TIMBER BY SANDING DOWN

MM. DIAM. TIMBER DOWELS SPACED OMM. APART MAXIMUM

OPENING WIDTH LESS 10MM.

800MM.

SIDE RAILS GLUED AND CLAMPED TO TOP & BOTTOM RAILS

CORNER DETAIL

DRILL FOR AND INSERT TWO 6MM. DIAM DOWELS THROUGH SIDE RAILS INTO TOP & BOTTOM RAILS

DOWEL SET APPROX. 25MM. INTO RAILS

DRESSED TIMBER BATTENS SPACED APART 5MM. WIDER THAN FRAME

BATTENS SCREWED TO WALL OR DOOR FRAME BATTENS NOT LESS THAN 20 x 20MM. DRESSED SIZE

Having read the litany of safety and security problems to be faced by an average homeowner, who could be blamed for running, screaming, out into the garden to seek some relief!

SAFETY OUTDOORS

Make your garden hazard free

Special precautions are necessary outdoors, especially if you have young children or an elderly relative living or staying with you.

Sadly, the great outdoors has its share of great and small problems, particularly if you have young children, a large garden, a pool or a garage/ workroom.

PLANT PERILS

Have you moved into a house that has poisonous (to animals and children) flowers or shrubs in the garden? Have you unwittingly planted some yourself? There aren't many, you'll be relieved to know, but if your botanical knowledge is on the sketchy side, it's probably worth a visit to your local library, gardening club or nursery, to get some information on the poisonous plants that thrive in or are native to your area, or to check the identity of any unfamiliar plant in your garden.

MACHINE MENACES

Lawn mowers must have been invented by a sadomasochist! Mowing can be exceptionally dangerous unless you are wearing the right footwear. Keep children, pets and yourself away

from flying stones, avoid hoses and built-in sprinklers – it all makes those push-pull mowers of yesteryear look very attractive, not to mention good for shedding a little extra weight! Never add fuel to a mower when it's hot as the fuel may ignite.

Machines for cutting back excess growth in difficult-to-reach spots (called by various names, including whipper-

snippers), can also be dangerous in inexperienced hands, and hedge trimmers even more so.

The key to safety when handling dangerous, bladed machinery – even a simple axe – is good maintenance. This includes oiling, sharpening and proper storage and a working knowledge of the machine's limitations as well as your own!

Wearing ear defenders when operating shrill machinery and wearing goggles to protect your eyes from splintering debris are practical precautions. Accidents occur every year which result in impaired hearing or sight after using such machines.

Other potential hazards encountered in the average garden include:

❋ Uneven pathways and natural stone steps that can cause falls.

❋ Slippery pathways are a hazard so when relaying a new path make sure that you choose a non-slip material.

❋ Tools left lying around carelessly for children to 'play' with, or for burglars to use in gaining access to your house.

❋ Insufficient outside lighting which can cause falls, and encourage would-be thieves looking for the cover darkness provides!

TOOLSHED TRAPS

❋ When doing any handy work make sure that the work area is as level as possible and that your tools are within reach so that you do not have to stretch for anything.

❋ Make sure you have a first aid kit close by.

❋ Never wear thongs or sandals when doing any do-it-yourself projects.

❋ Generally when using tools drive them away from you rather than towards you. That way, should anything slip, it will be moving away from you.

Children of all ages delight in outdoor play. Grass lawns create large, relatively soft expanses of area to play in

❋ Do not block off the ventilation slots in a power tool as it may overheat.

❋ When changing blades always make sure the tool is disconnected from the power source.

❋ Don't store flammable rubbish such as old paint tins, oily rags, newspapers, magazines or remnants of carpet.

BARBECUE BLISS

❋ Always have water close by and if you barbecue regularly it may be worthwhile having a fire extinguisher or fire blanket.

❋ Make sure children are kept away from the barbecue area and away from matches.

❋ Always use fire lighters to help start the fire – never use flammable liquids.

Special precautions are needed with sheds and garages. We look at play areas for children and examine the safety considerations necessary around water, including the serious responsibilities that come with pool ownership.

APL

An effective way of storing tools and potentially dangerous chemicals, is to make a wall cupboard with a child-resistant safety catch located out of reach of small children.

Project 12

Storage Cupboards

There's nothing like a little bit of a potter, away from the demands of the family. Your shed can be the haven where you put together the kinds of projects listed in this book. You may potter with pottery, and have a wheel and kiln out in your particular refuge. Your shed may be a shrine to gardening with secateurs, fertilisers and pesticides galore.

Capable people, who know what they're doing, are usually perfectly safe surrounded by their tools and implements, but others are not. It is a capable person's responsibility, therefore, to ensure that others, particularly children, cannot get at anything potentially dangerous.

The project illustrated opposite deals with the making of a simple cupboard for the storage of tools, pesticides and specialist equipment. This is fabricated from plywood with timber battens at the top and bottom to take the weight. The door is useful for storing tools such as saws and chisels, and if the cupboard is located next to your workbench, these would be readily to hand when working. Adjustable shelves are useful for storing bulky tools such as wood planes, nail containers and chemicals such as adhesive and paint.

All the plywood panels should be glued with a PVA adhesive and screwed together with self-tapping screws. If screwing into the end grain of plywood, drill small pilot holes for the screws so that the plywood is not spread apart when driving home the screw.

SELF-CLOSING DOORS

Garage tool sheds and garden stores should have a self-closing door. The simplest way of making an existing door self-closing is to fit a spring at the top of the door. These are available from hardware stores and can be easily fitted to the door and frame. As an alternative, replace the door hinges with 'rising butt' or spring hinges, or fit a purpose-made door-closer.

WHAT TO BUY
- [ ] plywood, to dimensions indicated in diagram
- [ ] 75 mm x 25 mm planed battens (1 length x 2.4 m)
- [ ] 2 magnetic catches
- [ ] 1 child-proof catch
- [ ] adjustable shelf brackets
- [ ] 40 mm long self-tapping screws
- [ ] 3 of 75 mm butt hinges
- [ ] PVA adhesive (glue)

TOOLS
- [ ] power saw
- [ ] drill

TIME
Approximately 4-5 hours

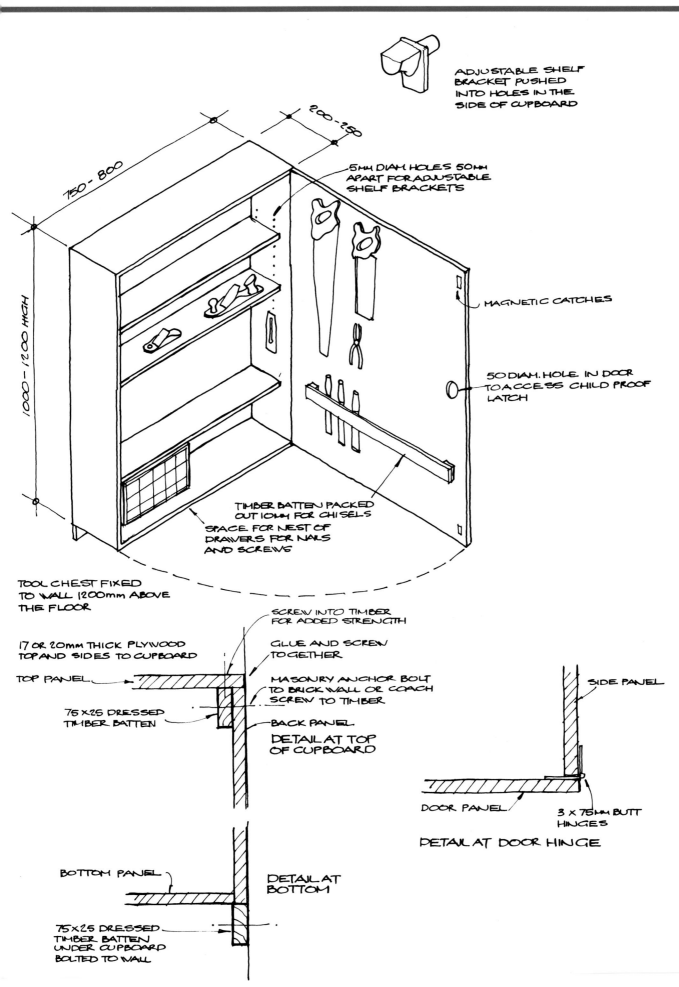

ADJUSTABLE SHELF BRACKET PUSHED INTO HOLES IN THE SIDE OF CUPBOARD

5MM DIAM HOLES 50MM APART FOR ADJUSTABLE SHELF BRACKETS

200 - 250

750 - 800

1000 - 1200 HIGH

MAGNETIC CATCHES

50 DIAM. HOLE IN DOOR TO ACCESS CHILD PROOF LATCH

TIMBER BATTEN PACKED OUT 10MM FOR CHISELS

SPACE FOR NEST OF DRAWERS FOR NAILS AND SCREWS

TOOL CHEST FIXED TO WALL 1200mm ABOVE THE FLOOR

SCREW INTO TIMBER FOR ADDED STRENGTH

GLUE AND SCREW TOGETHER

17 OR 20MM THICK PLYWOOD TOP AND SIDES TO CUPBOARD

TOP PANEL

MASONRY ANCHOR BOLT TO BRICK WALL OR COACH SCREW TO TIMBER

75 x 25 DRESSED TIMBER BATTEN

BACK PANEL

DETAIL AT TOP OF CUPBOARD

SIDE PANEL

DOOR PANEL

3 x 75MM BUTT HINGES

DETAIL AT DOOR HINGE

BOTTOM PANEL

DETAIL AT BOTTOM

75 x 25 DRESSED TIMBER BATTEN UNDER CUPBOARD BOLTED TO WALL

When planning a play area outside your house, remember that the smaller the children, the closer they should be to the house, preferably close to a window or glass door through which you can watch them.

PLAY AREAS

How to have fun the safe way

Children love the outdoors and thrive on sun and fresh air. Make your garden and outdoor area safe for them to play in and generally child-friendly.

Although your garden and outdoor area may seem like a safe place for children, the chances are there are many hazards. Regularly comb the area for objects that could be dangerous, such as broken glass, rope, barbecue equipment and gardening tools

E. Stone/APL

I f you can't see your children, make sure you can hear them. There is no more ominous a noise than silence, where small children are concerned.

As soon as your children are able to understand, teach them to recognise potentially dangerous situations and objects such as broken glass on the grass.

We have included some important outdoor safety guidelines.

SAFETY POINTERS

❊ Skateboards, tricycles, bikes and roller skates need a paved area, preferably on a slight incline, so keep this in mind too. Don't allow your children to play with wheeled toys on your driveway. They could be run over by a visitor unaware of 'their territory'.

❊ Many very young children these days spend at least some time in playgroups, where painting, pasting, making collages and generally making a huge mess is sanctioned. Why not allow this kind of activity outdoors at your place? Non-toxic paints and glues are totally safe these days.

❊ Other great fun, messy activities include the making of mud pies and playing with the garden hose on hot days.

❊ Fences are vital for retaining young children, and a two metre high fence is not too extreme.

❊ Around any pool, or garden pond there should also be child-proof fencing

with a child-proof latch at the top of the gate. These can be frustrating for adults to use, but make sure you don't fall for the temptation of propping the gate open.

❊ Balconies and verandahs are common play areas for children, especially those who live in a block of flats. It is imperative to fix high railings which cannot be climbed, in both cases.

❊ Make sure any apparatus and free-standing swings are very well anchored. Your little ones may not tip them up, but larger visiting cousins could.

❊ Wood chips and sand are both good for making inevitable falls less painful, so place them under slippery dips, see-saws, swings, climbing frames and so on.

❊ Favour soft materials. For instance, make your swing seats out of canvas, plastic or from an old tyre. Children are always being hit on their heads by swing seats, so try to minimise the pain.

❊ Small children need to be protected from the elements, so you might like to kill two birds with one stone and construct a wendy house or fort for them to play in and to seek protection in. Many mail-order houses can send out kits these days but make sure you enquire whether or not the wood has been impregnated with insecticides or other toxic material before you buy.

❊ Make sure the wood

used in your child's play structure is good quality, smooth and with rounded edges, not a splintery seconds-type quality. From time to time check the wood for splinters.

❊ A favourite for all children is the sandpit. It is also one of the safest pieces of play equipment.

❊ Every now and then you should check that the equipment is holding up and that the sandpit is clean (get a cat-proof, rain-proof cover for it as a matter of course). Also check regularly that any sandpit toys have not broken, causing sharp edges or broken off pieces that could be swallowed by a small child.

Toys that are suitable for the sandpit can include buckets, spades, scoops, tumblers and bottles – all made of plastic of course!

❊ If your incinerator or barbecue is near the play area, be very careful about storage of matches, fire lighters and so on, and

make sure all fires are completely put out before leaving the area.

❊ Compost and household rubbish are often stored outside, so keep your children's play area as far as possible from these sources of danger. A little chicken wire around the bins could help.

Remember that all timber used in projects of this nature should be treated with preservative if it is to stay outdoors. Even though children take to climbing naturally and are as agile as monkeys, safety has to come first with any climbing frame.

Child's Climbing Bridge

The climbing bridge illustrated is an example only and can be modified to your own special requirements. You may, for instance, want to suspend an old car tyre underneath, or attach a rope ladder on the side.

The first and most obvious safety consideration is the ground cover underneath the structure. If a child falls it should be onto sand or a surface like pine bark shavings – not concrete.

All the timber should be preservative-impregnated timber, usually pine. This treatment is common for children's outdoor playing equipment and wendy houses. Look in your telephone book for suppliers of this timber. Bolts, nails and the post spikes are available from hardware stores.

STEP BY STEP

1 Cut all poles to length, allowing for the depth into the footing. Lay the poles beside each other and mark the location of the main sidebeams on all poles. Use a saw and chisel to cut a 15 mm deep recess in each beam to take the beams. Bolt the beams to the poles with two galvanised coach bolts with washers at each pole.

2 Dig the holes for the poles, preferably using a hole borer to save effort. Lift the poles, with the main beams attached, into the holes and temporarily prop in a vertical

position with spare timber. Check that the main beams are level, packing under the poles with pieces of brick or stone if necessary to level the beams.

3 Make up some ready-mixed concrete to fill the holes. Manufacturers of ready-mixed concrete usually indicate how much concrete each bag will make. Leave the concrete for several days to allow it to cure adequately before proceeding to complete the bridge.

4 Once the pole uprights are set in concrete it is a simple matter of fixing the planks to the bridge, ladder and stair as indicated. The post spikes to the base of the stair should be set in concrete when the stair is complete.

WHAT TO BUY
- [ ] 70 mm diameter CCA-treated pine logs, 5 of 2 m long
- [ ] 90 mm x 30 mm, 8 of 2.7 m long
- [ ] 140 mm x 40 mm, 2 of 1.8 m long
- [ ] 90 mm x 40 mm, 2 of 2.4 m long, 1 of 3.0 m long
- [ ] ready-mixed concrete, 4 bags
- [ ] coach bolts, 10 of 125 mm long x 10 mm
- [ ] coach screws, 16 of 75 mm long
- [ ] nails, 75 mm long x 3.75 mm galvanised (2 kg)
- [ ] 2 galvanised steel post spikes

TOOLS
- [ ] post-hole borer (hire)
- [ ] power saw
- [ ] electric drill

TIME
Approximately two days plus curing time for concrete

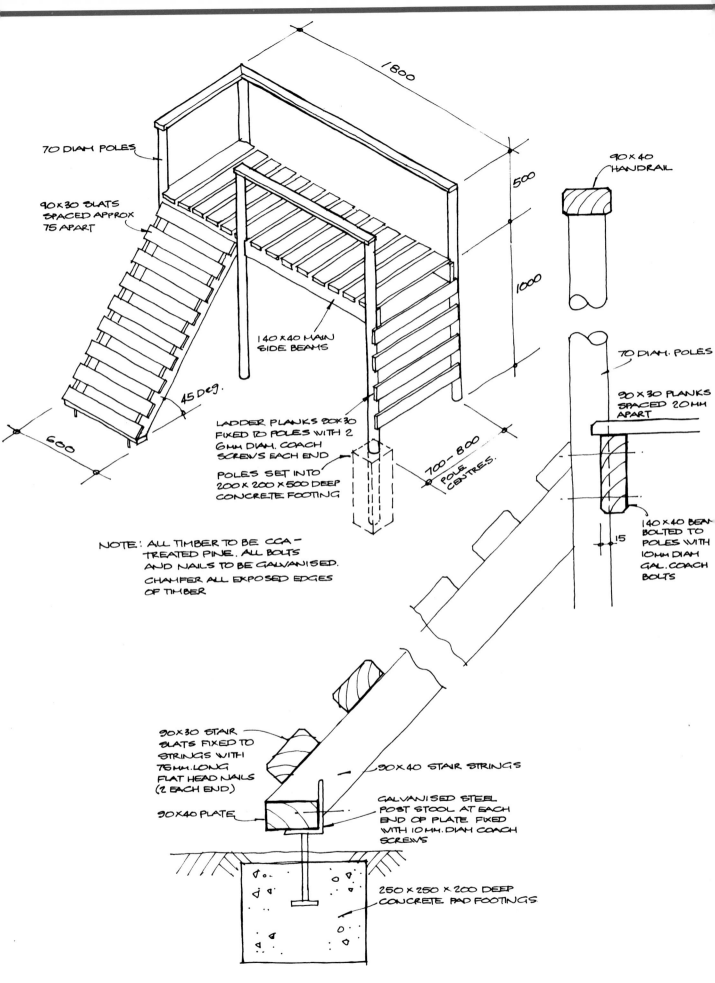

70 DIAM POLES

90 x 30 SLATS
SPACED APPROX
75 APART

1800

500

1000

90 x 40
HANDRAIL

70 DIAM. POLES

90 x 30 PLANKS
SPACED 20 MM
APART

140 x 40 MAIN
SIDE BEAMS

45 Deg.

600

LADDER PLANKS 90 x 30
FIXED TO POLES WITH 2
6 MM DIAM. COACH
SCREWS EACH END

POLES SET INTO
200 x 200 x 500 DEEP
CONCRETE FOOTING

700 - 800
POLE
CENTRES.

140 x 40 BEAM
BOLTED TO
POLES WITH
10MM DIAM
GAL. COACH
BOLTS

15

NOTE: ALL TIMBER TO BE CCA -
TREATED PINE. ALL BOLTS
AND NAILS TO BE GALVANISED.
CHAMFER ALL EXPOSED EDGES
OF TIMBER

90 x 30 STAIR
SLATS FIXED TO
STRINGS WITH
75 MM. LONG
FLAT HEAD NAILS
(2 EACH END)

90 x 40 PLATE

90 x 40 STAIR STRINGS

GALVANISED STEEL
POST STOOL AT EACH
END OF PLATE FIXED
WITH 10 MM. DIAM COACH
SCREWS

250 x 250 x 200 DEEP
CONCRETE PAD FOOTINGS.

Children love to have their own special place to play in, and a wendy house, whether on the ground, elevated on a platform or in a tree, is one of the most popular private domains for a child.

Project 14

Wendy House

This wendy house is a fun project for a child-safe play area. If you don't want to make your own, they can be bought in kit form from specialist companies. It is best to use preservative-treated timbers, usually pine.

A child discovering the world around him through play

Benn Mitchell/The Image Bank

The wendy house illustrated is intended to be built at ground level, although the same design could be raised above the ground by using longer poles. All bolt fixings should be zinc-plated and all nails galvanised.

STEP BY STEP

1 Set out the bearers on bricks making sure these are level. Nail the joists over the bearers and skew nail to the top of the bearers.

2 The poles should be trenched at the bottom where they butt into the bearers. This means they are cut out.

3 Stand the poles in place and fix to the bearers with coach screws. Temporarily brace plumb. Fix the planed beams to the poles on each side, together with the flooring panels.

4 The roof frames should be pre-fabricated at ground level and then nailed to the beams.

5 The side frames and linings should now be erected as they act as bracing. If you don't want lattice panels, diagonal cross braces will do equally well.

6 Lay roofing planks starting from the edges and overlapping about 30 mm.

WHAT TO BUY

- ☐ 11 of 75 mm x 50 mm rafters x 2.4 m long
- ☐ 4 of 150 mm x 50 mm planed beam x 2.4 m long
- ☐ 5 of 100 mm x 50 mm sawn joists x 3 m long
- ☐ 5 of 100 mm x 25 mm planed x 2.4 m long
- ☐ 4 of 70 mm diam. poles x 2.4 m long
- ☐ 2 sheets of 18 mm thick plywood x 2.4 m long x 0.9 m wide
- ☐ 18 of 150 mm x 12 mm roof boards x 2.1 m long
- ☐ 16 of 10 mm coach screws
- ☐ lattice panels, to suit area required
- ☐ 1 galvanised ridge cap, 2.1 m long

TOOLS

- ☐ power saw and drill
- ☐ hammer
- ☐ spanner
- ☐ spirit level

TIME

Approximately 8 hours

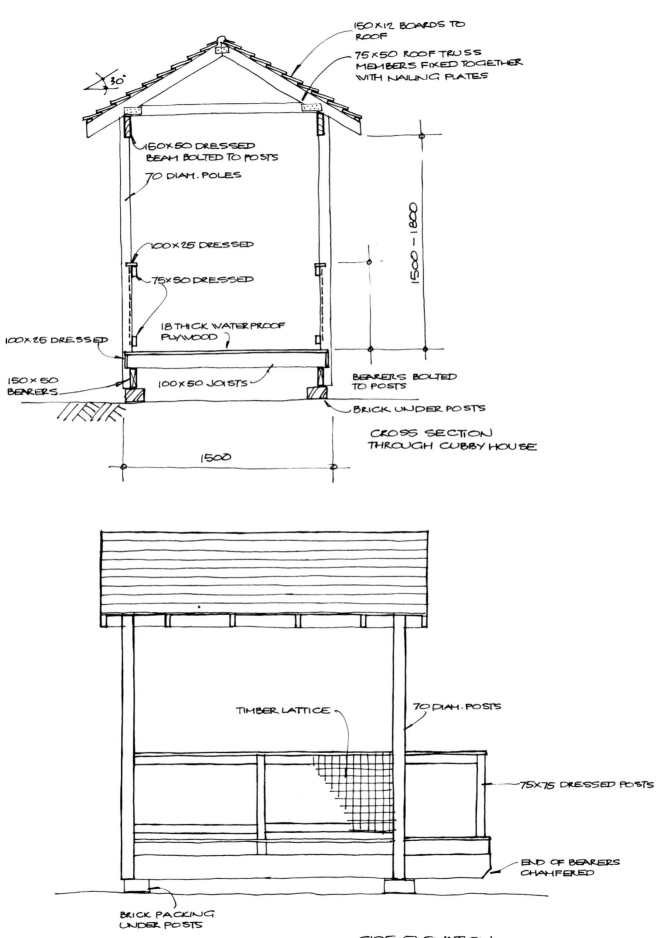

150 X 12 BOARDS TO ROOF

75 X 50 ROOF TRUSS MEMBERS FIXED TOGETHER WITH NAILING PLATES

30°

150 X 50 DRESSED BEAM BOLTED TO POSTS

70 DIAM. POLES

100 X 25 DRESSED

75 X 50 DRESSED

18 THICK WATERPROOF PLYWOOD

100 X 25 DRESSED

150 X 50 BEARERS

100 X 50 JOISTS

1500 – 1800

BEARERS BOLTED TO POSTS

BRICK UNDER POSTS

CROSS SECTION THROUGH CUBBY HOUSE

1500

TIMBER LATTICE

70 DIAM. POSTS

75 X 75 DRESSED POSTS

END OF BEARERS CHAMFERED

BRICK PACKING UNDER POSTS

SIDE ELEVATION

A play shop is another one of those all-time favourites where children are concerned, perhaps because it has the potential to become anything they want it to be — the neighbourhood corner shop or supermarket, a castle, a cave or a space ship for example.

Project 15

Play Shop

The little shop illustrated is an all-purpose play structure which could be used as a puppet theatre, or anything children wish to make of it. Use preservative-treated timber and galvanised bolts and nails should be galvanised to prevent corrosion.

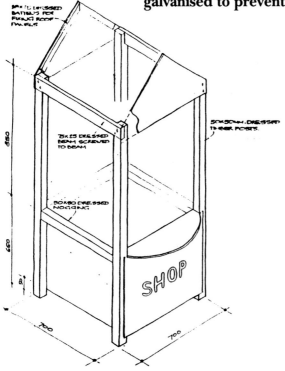

5 All that remains is to fix the roof panels. Make sure that the frames are square to each other, using a try square and checking that the diagonal dimensions are the same, before measuring the size of the roof panels and fixing in position.

6 Glue and screw planed timber battens to the inside of the gable panels, as indicated (see diagram), for fixing the roof panels. The roof panels are screwed to the top of the gable panels, the side beams and the batten at the ridge, with 25 mm self-tapping screws at 150 mm centres. Cut out the counter top and screw to the top of the front nogging.

7 Make sure that all sharp edges of the timber are planed or sanded down. The completed structure can now be painted to your colour scheme.

STEP BY STEP

1 The sequence of work starts with making the two side frames. Cut all the posts to the same size and rebate the top to take the top beam. Screw the top beams in place.

2 Cut the noggings to fit between the posts and fix in place by nailing through the posts. The side plywood panels can then be nailed in place. Use round head nails 25 mm long, spaced 150 mm apart.

3 Stand the two side frames and temporarily prop upright. Nail in place the front and back noggings.

4 The next stage is to fix the front plywood panel and the gable panels. Make sure that the posts are vertical before fixing these in place with cheese-head countersunk screws 25 mm long, driven into small pilot holes.

WHAT TO BUY
- [ ] 5 of 50 mm x 50 mm planed posts and noggings, 2.1 m long
- [ ] 75 mm x 25 mm planed beam, 1.8m long
- [ ] 38 mm x 25 mm planed battens, 2.1 m long
- [ ] 1 sheet of 6 mm thick plywood (exterior grade), 2.4 m x 1.2 m
- [ ] zinc-plated screws
- [ ] 25 mm long round head nails

TOOLS
- [ ] power saw
- [ ] drill
- [ ] try square

TIME
Approximately 6-8 hours

Pools, lakes, rivers, dams, the sea, storm water drains, canals all share one thing in common, aside from water. It's danger. Children and adults who are weak swimmers, or who do not swim at all, must observe safety procedures and treat water with the respect it deserves.

WATER WAYS

Children are always drawn to water

Too many accidents, many fatal, occur in water – even in the most apparently 'safe' situations. You can never be too vigilant where water safety is concerned.

Follow our safety guidelines to help you and your family relax by the pool.

✻ Make a point of teaching the basics of treading water and dog paddle to young children as soon as they are capable of understanding you.

✻ Learn resuscitation techniques, including CPR (cardio-pulmonary resuscitation), teach others resuscitation techniques and buy a large, bright chart of resuscitation steps to hang beside your pool or spa, indoors or out.

✻ Adults should not drink alcohol or eat heavy meals before swimming.

✻ Keep anything glass or electrical out of the pool area.

✻ Keep a first aid kit near the pool.

✻ Supervision of children around all types of water, including the humble bath, must be constant.

✻ Just as children should be taught never to run riot in the bathroom, so should they be taught never to run around a swimming pool area. This is easier said than done

but slippery surfaces *are* extremely dangerous. Unfortunately one mishap or accident is usually the best teacher.

✻ Consider buying a sturdy easy-to-use pool cover. Pool covers keep leaves and other debris out of your pool so are best used every day.

✻ Pool alarms are now widely available. The alarm will ring if anything over the weight of a twig falls into the pool. In a household filled with young children, an alarm could help ease the burden of constant vigilance.

✻ A fine mesh of wire or material over a fishpond is a good idea if there are young children around.

✻ Difficult children or 'bolters' must be made to wear a flotation device in and out of the water when playing by the pool.

✻ Have something handy – even if it's just a leaf scooper or stick – to hold out to a person in difficulty. A lifebuoy by a pool is useful too, as are flotation toys. If you jump in to water which is out of your depth to help a

panicking person, you risk being drowned yourself. Jump in to rescue a child if you are able to stand at that depth.

✻ Don't swim in the sea alone, even if you are a champion swimmer.

✻ Assess depth with a stick, or by walking into the water, before you take it upon yourself to dive in.

✻ Lock pool chlorine and other chemicals away until they are needed.

✻ Leaf skimmer boxes and other filtering devices can be dangerous, so make sure children cannot get at them.

✻ In-pool vacuuming machines have been known to suck in long hair, thereby holding a child's head underwater. Turn them off and take them out of the pool when it is in use.

✳ Keep pool water clean and clear to minimise the risk of ear and other infections.

✳ If more than one child is to be watched, more than one adult is needed for supervision.

✳ Complete the 'Emergency Telephone List' on page 30 and keep it in a safe place readily accessible to the outdoor area.

✳ Do not leave any brightly coloured toys floating in the pool as a toddler may be tempted to reach out and fall in.

Constant attention is essential in preventing drowning accidents. Special care is needed in rivers and creeks especially, and children should never be allowed to swim without responsible adult supervision and the normal water safety precautions

✳ Never allow children to ride bikes near the pool's edge.

✳ Small paddling pools should always be emptied when not in use.

✳ Ensure that the pool area is fenced off with a child-proof latch on the gate and choose a fence that has no toeholds in the framing.

Children have a fascination for water and it is a source of important creative play

The fence around a pool or spa must be as close to unclimbable as possible, but some smart-alecky three-year-olds can climb absolutely anything.

Project 16

Child-proof Gate Latches

Below are two examples of safety latches available. The diagram shows a system which can be easily installed. This relies on the strength required to pull against the spring as the principle means of security.

Make sure that you regularly check safety latches on your pool fence gate. These can become weakened over time so it's important to check for any signs of rust or wear.

The other system is commonly used for metal gates around swimming pools and is more difficult to install. The inexper- ienced do-it-yourselfer may be well advised to get help from a professional when it comes to installation. Follow our instructions for installing a child-proof latch.

STEP BY STEP

1 Fix hinges to gate following instructions supplied with the hinge set. Make sure that the gate swings freely and easily.

2 Mark the location and screw fix the latch in position. Again make sure that the latch closes easily. Adjust the position of the latch if necessary.

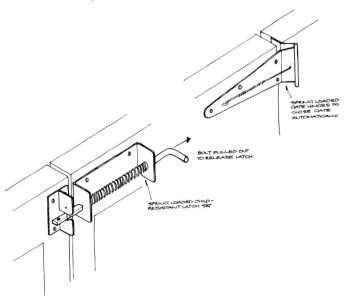

This shows one of many recognised methods of child-proofing the closure on your swimming pool fence. The only way this gate can be opened is for the nob on the post to be twisted, thus releasing a catch lower down. You need to be adult size to achieve this, and there is no way a child could climb the fence as the cross rails are deliberately designed to be well apart

WHAT TO BUY

☐ latch set and spring hinges complete with screws (from hardware stores)

TOOLS

☐ drill
☐ screwdriver

TIME

Approximately 1-2 hours

During an emergency, there is usually no time to sit around and think rationally about what you should do. A panic reaction will worsen a crisis and must be avoided at all costs. You must act, and quickly.

EMERGENCIES

Dealing with a crisis situation

Even if you take every security and safety precaution listed in this book, you are still likely to encounter an unforeseen emergency. It's better to work out what you would do before it happens, rather than while it's happening! Here, we offer some advice in emergency situations like fires, burns, poisoning, choking, heart attack and drowning. Remember, however, that it is also important, wherever possible, to get professional help to the scene of an accident very quickly.

Serious outcomes can be reduced if you know how to handle an emergency correctly.

Keep our 'Emergency Telephone List' on page 30 handy.

CHOKING
Signs to watch for include a coughing fit, alarming attempts to breathe, throat clutching and a growing blueness over the lips, face and nail beds.

If conscious, have the person relax, breathe deeply and cough to remove the object. If breathing is difficult, seek medical aid. If breathing and unconscious, turn the person to the side and seek medical aid. If the person is not breathing, lay him or her down, keeping the head low and give three or four sharp blows between the shoulder blades and get medical attention immediately.

FIRE
Tell children to get down on the floor, crawl to the bedroom or exit door and feel the door knob. If it is hot, don't open the door. Start crawling towards a window.

Never throw water on oil fires, such as a pan of cooking chips. These fires must be smothered.

Keep fire blankets, mini-extinguishers and so on close at hand in high risk areas. They are no use to you if thrown into the back of an inaccessible pot cupboard.

If the fire is out of control and you are unable to deal with it, close all windows and doors, turn off the electric power at the meter box outside, call the fire brigade and evacuate.

Work out an escape route from your home, based on the assumption that the fire has started in the kitchen. Then work out alternative routes based on the assumption that you can't leave by the back door or by the front door. Make instructions simple for children.

Have fire drills and rehearse the routes. Don't tell them to wait in their rooms until you come. You may have been overcome by smoke.

Forget property – protect other people and yourself first.

BURNS

Put out burning clothing by making the victim roll onto a rug or blanket or by using water.

Cut burnt clothing off, very gently but swiftly. If any clothing is stuck to the skin, leave it.

The burnt area should be cooled under gently running water for up to 10 minutes.

Bandage badly burnt areas (use a clean sheet or pillowcase, if nothing else is available) and, if still very painful, continue to pour water over the bandaged wound.

The victim will require medical attention as soon as possible.

POISONING

A small child suffering from poisoning will have one or more of the following symptoms or signs:
- ☐ burning pains, particularly around the mouth and throat areas
- ☐ nausea
- ☐ stomach pain
- ☐ drowsiness or disorientation
- ☐ difficulty in breathing
- ☐ blue lips
- ☐ vomiting

If the victim can speak, or communicate in some way, try to find out what has been ingested or inhaled, or what has bitten them. Find out how long before.

Take any empty tablet bottles, pesticide or cleaning containers, or whatever else seems to be the cause of the poisoning with you to the hospital for analysis.

Do not induce vomiting if the victim has taken something corrosive (like dishwashing powder) or petroleum-based (like kerosene). Do not force the person to walk around if drowsy as this will cause the poisonous substance to circulate faster.

As soon as the victim is stabilised phone the Poisons Information Service number (keep the number by the phone, for further instructions. If victim's breathing or pulse goes, start resuscitation procedures straight away.

Get professional medical help as soon as possible.

HEART ATTACK AND DROWNING

Cardio-pulmonary resuscitation (CPR) involves breathing into a victim's lungs via the mouth or nose while alternatively pressing on the heart. This pressure keeps the blood circulating, which in turn keeps the victim's brain alive. There is not a second to lose as brain

death occurs in just a few minutes.

Start CPR if the carotid pulse (each side of the neck) does not respond and after clearing the airway give four or five full, but fast, breaths via artificial respiration techniques.

Kneel with one knee in line with the victim's chest and the other level with the head. Leave one index finger at the base of the sternum and put the heel of your other hand just above this point, making sure you are keeping to the middle of the sternum, not off centre. Place one hand on top of the other. Using your body weight as the force, push through the heel of the lower hand. Your shoulders should be vertical over the breastbone of the victim.

Don't thump. Compress rhythmically. The breastbone of an adult should be depressed a few centimetres with each compression.

After 15 or so compressions (done in around 10 or 12 seconds) try to fit in two breaths into the victim's lungs within the next three to five seconds, via artificial respiration.

Obviously if somebody is with you, they can do the breathing while you do the compressions. In this case, try one breath by person A for every five compressions by person B.

When performing CPR on children, aim to depress the breastbone about two centimetres, 100 times per minute. For babies under 12 months of age, depress one centimetre, otherwise proceed as with children.

Make a point of seeing CPR demonstrated on adult and child size dummies or ask a trained person to show you how it's done. One day you may be glad you did.

FIREARMS

If you are one of the small number of people who possess firearms follow these safety rules to avoid

You should always keep a basic first aid kit in your house fully stocked. Always anticipate where and how an emergency might occur.

◼ Salt and sodium bicarbonate solution to induce vomiting, but seek medical advice before giving this.

◼ An antiseptic liquid and cotton wool balls.

◼ A pair of square-ended tweezers small enough to remove fine splinters and so on.

◼ A pair of scissors, for cutting bandages or plasters and burnt clothes.

◼ A selection of bandages, sticking plasters and lint.

◼ A hot/cold pack for strains, sprains and even childbirth pains!

◼ Pins and slings, for securing bandages and making them stay on.

◼ A small pack of alcohol rubs, for quick sterilising of a needle or a thermometer.

◼ A thermometer.

◼ A medicine measure.

◼ Infant's and children's liquid paracetamol.

◼ A treatment for rashes, itchy skin conditions and sunburn like Calamine Lotion.

◼ A cooling anti-inflammatory preparation for stings.

◼ A syringe, minus the needle, for getting medicines down reluctant throats.

◼ Some small sweets in an airtight container can be good first aid with small children! Change these regularly to make sure they are edible when you need them!

tragic accidents.

✳ Assume every firearm is loaded until you open the action and prove to yourself that it isn't. When your gun is not in use make sure it is not loaded and that the safety catch is on.

✳ Never climb any fence or wall while holding a loaded firearm. Disarm it and carry it or ask some-one to pass it up.

✳ Store unloaded firearms in locked cupboards and separate from ammunition.

A first aid kit is essential for every home. Be sure to keep it in an accessible position where everyone in the family can find it easily and quickly. It's a good idea to keep a spare kit in the garage or garden shed – it may be quicker to reach when accidents happen outside the home

You don't have to be a card-carrying Greenie to want a home environment that's as free of polluting chemicals and waste as possible. These days, that's just about everybody's aim.

HOME SWEET HOME
Create an environment-friendly home

Few homes have been untouched or unmoved by recent information about dangerous pesticides, the need to recycle, the importance of finding substitutes for unnecessary chemicals in cleaning

products, and so on. Sometimes, however, the big issues of ozone layer depletion, heavy metal pollution, vast oil spills and the rest make us feel unable to contribute to change.

The fact is that we can all contribute to fixing the big picture by starting at home, with the small picture.

In this section we're going to look at hidden pollution dangers around

Some hazards around the home remain well hidden and difficult to deal with. Allergies caused by pollutants in the air or dust mites are an example of this. Toxic fumes, garden pesticides and insulation materials can all cause harmful effects.

73

the house, how to keep and use pesticides safely and what chemicals can be substituted with natural alternatives. We also look at how to dispose of wastes and recycling.

POLLUTION DANGERS

Allergic reactions, asthma attacks, respiratory infections and a variety of other major and minor health problems can result from pollutants that are in the air at home.

Cigarette, Pipe and Cigar Smoke

More people are now aware of the problems inherent in passive smoking. They are also increasingly aware that smoking around small children and babies can increase the children's incidence of illness, including coughs that refuse to get better, ear infections and a variety of respiratory illnesses. Developing bronchial tissue does not need smoke!

Dust Mites

These microscopic mites, which tend to live in bedding and carpets, have been squarely blamed for many allergic reactions. Special sprays and mattress covers can be a great help in reducing irritation caused by mites.

Home Heating

It has recently come to light that proper ventilation is essential in rooms where gas and other heaters are merrily burning away. Counter-productive as it may sound, it is recommended that a window be open in such rooms at all times so that polluting elements, including carbon monoxide, don't build up into high concentrations.

Wood-burning stoves have an extra problem – their emissions can be irritating to the respiratory tract tissue of adults and children. This irritation is more damaging to children's developing lungs.

A non-polluting and money-saving solution to being cold in winter is to cut off draughts around your doors, draw heavy curtains across your windows, and simply put more clothes on!

Humidifiers

In homes where flu-prone young children live, it is often suggested that a humidifier, also known as a vaporiser, be turned on in the child's room while he or she sleeps. These appliances add moisture to the air which helps the child breathe more easily. The main worry with these is that they are very easy to tip over, and could be responsible for nasty burns. Secondly, micro-organisms can grow in these appliances if they are not cleaned out every day – a fact few parents are aware of. The bacteria that can enter the air, if the appliance is not cleaned, has been linked with a form of sickness that resembles pneumonia.

Toxic Fumes

The dangers of lead paint are well known, but lead can also enter the house via petrol fumes from your car, and through the door that connects your garage and your home. Seal connecting doors properly and have the garage door open while 'warming the engine'. Use lead-free fuel if your car can run on it.

Don't burn plastics as they release poisonous fumes.

Building Materials

A most dangerous material used in buildings, particularly those constructed before the 1950s, is asbestos. If you suspect it is present between your walls or on your pipes, get it checked immediately. Don't continue any renovations or removal of it. It is lethal, over a period of time, so should be removed by professionals. To summarise, good ventilation is a must. Remember to air your home as often as possible. Also remember to clean air conditioners and exhaust fan filters regularly, so that bugs don't proliferate and go around for a second or third time!

Using Pesticides

First and foremost, you should keep pesticides in the containers they originally came in and they should be locked away out of children's reach. Never put pesticides in soft drink bottles!

Some pesticides are dangerous when inhaled, so be careful when spraying. A mask may be necessary. Good ventilation is important if you're spraying indoors.

For pesticides you have to mix yourself, only make up as much as you need at that time, no more. Be familiar with first aid procedure so you know what action to take if a child has managed to swallow some or get it onto skin or into eyes.

Don't kill ants with an elephant gun! Know which pesticide, and how much of it, is appropriate for the job at hand. Never spray near pets' drink or food bowls, or near children's toys and other gear.

There are a thousand and one things that will recycle in some way or another, and it is in your interest, as well as the environment, to begin recycling as much as you can.

RECYCLING
Safe and secure means environment-friendly

Recycling is an essential part of being a conservationist, and making the world a safer, healthier place.

Paper is perhaps the most obvious thing we think of when the word 'recycling' is used, but here are some other recycling possibilities to put into practise.

Aluminium Cans – These recycle very well and in some instances you will be paid for bringing in certain weights of them.

Glass Bottles – Recycle these by using the bottle bank nearest you.

Glass Milk Bottles – These can keep doing the rounds for ages.

Plastic Bags – Re-use these as often as possible. Take your own shopping bag or basket to the supermarket and refuse the new batch of plastic bags offered.

Paper Bags – These can often be re-used for children's school lunches, storage and so on.

Gift Wrapping – This can be trimmed and ironed to be as good as new. For children's birthday presents, use one of the many 'art works' brought home by your child from school for gift wrap.

Aluminium Foil – Pieces of foil can be re-used many times over.

The Right Frame of Mind

One classic example of a recycling mentality in action: babies' clothes and gear. We all know how quickly babies grow out of their clothes and a first-time mother would literally never have to buy so much as a bootie if she didn't want to, because she will be swamped with offers of clothes, buggies, cots, changing tables – everything! Why not translate this thinking into more aspects of everyday life?

✱ Recycle broken goods which you may be tempted to throw out. Have them repaired instead.

✱ Give away or sell unwanted things – you never know what someone else may find useful.

✱ Use old toothbrushes to clean difficult spots, like the bases of taps.

✱ Buy second-hand goods, furniture, toys and so on yourself.

✳ Separate your refuse into recyclable and non-recyclable components and lobby local authorities to arrange collections in your area of recyclable goods.

✳ 'Recycle' food by starting a compost heap. If you have no garden, offer to supply someone else's compost near you.

✳ Re-use envelopes and other hardly used paper.

✳ Glossy magazines and books can be sent off to local nursing homes or hospitals, or to schools so that children can cut out the pictures for their art works.

✳ Mascara will 'recycle' after the wand is left in hot water for five minutes.

Eco-friendly Cleaners

Many heavy-duty household cleaning chemicals are often expensive, ecologically unsound and unnecessary. Lemons, sodium bicarbonate, hot water

and some physical effort will conquer most cleaning jobs around the home. Here are some cleaning tips and substitutes for the over-packaged, well-advertised mainstream cleaners:

✳ To keep drains free-flowing, avoid putting oil or grease down there at any time. Clean with vinegar (one cup) and sodium bicarbonate (a couple of heaped tablespoons). You put the sodium bicarbonate down first, then the vinegar and then you pour boiling water on top of that.

✳ Rub lemon over marks on ceramic tiles. Wait a few minutes, wipe with a dry cloth and see them sparkle.

✳ Clean inside your microwave by boiling up a bowl of water containing some slices of lemon. When the steam subsides, wipe down the oven walls.

✳ Clean inside a conventional oven by

putting a bowl of ammonia in the oven, leaving it overnight, then wiping down the oven's interior. Grease will come off very easily. Make sure the kitchen is well aired overnight.

✳ Clean stainless steel with a damp cloth that has been dipped in sodium bicarbonate.

✳ Window cleaners? It's hard to go past good old dampened newspaper. Dry the windows with a dry sheet of newspaper.

✳ Pure soap or soap flakes do just as good a job as harsh powders or liquid detergents. Make your own washing powder with one cup of soap flakes combined with half a cup of washing soda. Also see the Tipstrip on page 74 for a non-toxic all-purpose cleaner.

✳ Soak a cotton wool ball with a few drops of your favourite natural flower oil to keep the bathroom smelling great.

Also see the Tipstrip on page 74

TIPSTRIP

Try recycling food – and that doesn't mean eating leftovers!

■ Keep butter wrappers because they make great liners for cake tins and are useful for greasing trays.

■ Kindling for the fire comes from some unlikely sources, but did you know that dried potato peelings are good kindling?

■ Old tea leaves in warm water make a great wash for wooden floors. The colour improves and scum lifts off.

■ Apples, oranges and onions are often sold in those little mesh bags. Fill these with old scraps of soap, tie tightly and you have instant pan scourers.

■ After you've boiled eggs or vegetables, don't throw the boiled water down the sink. Wait until it cools then use it on your pot plants, herb box and hanging baskets.

Glossary

Batten: Thin timber member supporting sheets or coverings.

Casement windows: Side-hung window sashes.

CCA: Chrome Copper Arsenic, used to treat timber for prevention of rot and insect attack.

Coach bolts: Bolts with a domed head.

Coach screws: Large screws with a hexagonal head, requiring a spanner to turn into place.

Double-hung windows: Window with two separately hung sashes at the top and bottom which slide up and down.

Dowel: Round timber.

Framing anchors: Galvanised steel plates which are nailed to timber frames.

Hardcore: Crushed rock sub-base under roads and paving.

Hopper windows: Top-hung window sashes.

Joists: Timber floor frame onto which floor boards are nailed.

Masonry anchors: Steel bolts with sides which expand in the wall as the bolts are tightened.

Nailing plates: Galvanised steel plate with sections of the plate punched out to form nails. The plates are hammered onto the face of timbers which are to be joined together.

Noggings: Horizontal wall frames fixed between the vertical studs.

Plasterboard: Prefabricated finishing sheet made of gypsum plaster faced with craft paper.

PVA adhesive: Water-based glue which is quick drying and clear finishing.

Polyurethane: A hard yet resilient coating commonly used for wear areas.

Post-hole borer: Similar to a spade but with two plates at the end to lift soil out of holes.

Post spikes: Galvanised steel for supporting posts off the ground.

String line: Any type of string, stretched between two points to mark the line of a wall or path to be built.

Timber studs (wall studs): Vertical wall framing member.

Toggle bolts: Type of bolts for use with hollow walls. Two types are available; spring toggles and gravity toggles. In both cases the toggles open behind the wall lining for fixing.

Trimming joists: Timber frame between the main joists.

CONVERSION TABLE

LENGTHS
1 mm approx $3/64$ inch
10 mm approx $3/8$ inch
25 mm approx 1 inch
230 mm approx 9 inches
820 mm approx 32 inches
2400 mm approx 8 feet
1 m approx 39 inches
1.8 m approx 6 feet
2.04 m - just under 7 feet
3 m approx 10 feet
VOLUMES
1 litre approx 1.8 pints
4.5 litres approx 1 gallon
AREA
1 sq m approx 1 sq yd
9.3 sq m approx 1 building square - 100 sq ft

* the conversions are soft

A to Z of safety.

A is for **alarms** which are as varied in type as in price tag. **Asbestos**, the culprit of the pre-1950s home insulation scene (watch out, renovators).

B is for **barriers**, imperative at the tops and bottoms of stairs when a toddler is learning to walk.

C is for **CPR** or cardio-pulmonary resuscitation. Sounds serious, and it is. Learn it as soon as you can. **Checklists** are vital for getting things organised and done. **Child-proofing cupboards** and other child-proofing suggestions fill this book. Get cracking!

D is sadly for **drowning**, which is preventable in so many cases. See our chapter on water safety. **Drugs** can be a problem for the elderly, whose memories are not what they were. We suggest ways to help.

E is for **emergencies**, which even the best regulated households have to face from time to time. Learn what to do! Also learn to respect **electricity**.

F is for **first aid** which is your responsibility to learn the rudiments of. **Fences** help ensure safety when young children are around. **Firearms** need constant vigilance.

G is for **garages**. An open, empty one is a dead giveaway of an empty house and an unlocked one can be filled with no-nos for young children. **Glass** should be kept out of pool areas, made shatterproof in windows and recycled where possible.

H is for **home, sweet home** which should be your safe haven. Avoid having your home and possessions ransacked, by reading our tips.

I is for **insurance**, which nobody understands and everybody needs.

J is for **jemmying**, the time-honoured way of getting a window open in a hurry for nefarious purposes.

K is for **kitchens**, where it's not just bad cooking that's the risk!

L is for **laminated glass**, which will save many a fall from becoming a disaster, and also often stops burglars in their tracks.

M is for **Medicines**. These must be kept safely locked away or at least out of reach of small children.

N is for your local **Neighbourhood Watch** scheme, the single most effective burglar deterrent of our time.

O is for **obvious** and that's how burglars see key-hiding places like in the meterbox, under the door mat, under a pot plant or in the letter box. Don't be so predictable!

P is for **pools** which are a great joy and an even greater danger if young children can get near them. See our pool fence Child-proof Latch project. **Prickly plants** are a good burglar deterrent around the sides of houses. **Photograph** your valuables and have a greater chance of getting them back if they are stolen.

Q is for **quick**, which is how you must act in an emergency like fire, choking or drowning.

R is for **recycling**, which we must all start doing something about in our everyday lives. **Radios** left on all day, a little too loudly, are another giveaway to burglars.

S is for **safety, security, stair guards, slip rails, safe storage** and is obviously the **star** letter of this book.

T is for **trampolines** which belong in circuses, not in your garden.

U is for **uneven surfaces** in houses, in garages, in gardens – a fall is inevitable.

V is for **variety of lifestyle** which makes an empty home less predictable and therefore more secure.

W is for **windows**, the burglar's favourite access point. Don't make it easy for them.

X is for **Xtra Careful**, which is what you must be if you want to keep your home and family safe and secure.

Y is for **youngsters** who rely on you to ensure their safety because they cannot do it themselves. Don't let them down.

Z is for **zealous** which is what you must be if you want to enjoy peace of mind and a **Safe and Secure** home.

Page references to Projects are printed in bold type.

ACKNOWLEDGEMENTS

In the course of putting this series of projects together, many people helped. Special thanks go to Robert Fuller of the Newcastle MBA, as well as the St John Ambulance, Danicar Wrought Iron and Hewi Australia.